DASH DIET 2024

FOR BEGINNERS

Your Essential Guide to Healthy Living and Weight Management

LION WEBER
PUBLISHING

Copyright © 2024 Lion Weber Publishing

Join our Facebook Group and get recipes for free:

Lion Meals Made Easy:
https://www.facebook.com/groups/1500151320483566

THANK YOU FOR YOUR PURCHASE!

By signing up for our newsletter,
you'll receive access to our exclusive

KETO RECIPE, ONE PAN RECIPEs, MUG MEAL RECIPE,

AIR FRYER RECIPE, and 5-INGREDIENT RECIPE.

These recipes are easy to follow
and perfect for busy individuals
who want to eat healthy
and delicious meals.

GET YOUR FREE GIFT NOW!

https://l.ead.me/lwp-free-gift

TABLE OF CONTENTS

Introduction

When embarking on a weight loss journey, seeking out a program or plan tailored to your needs and preferences is crucial. The ideal weight loss program not only helps you shed unwanted pounds but also prioritizes your health and well-being. Sustainable weight loss is gradual and consistent, typically averaging about one to two pounds weekly. Rapid weight loss may seem desirable but rarely leads to long-term success, as it can be challenging to maintain. Therefore, focusing on healthy habits and lifestyle changes that can be sustained over time is essential.

The DASH (Dietary Approaches to Stop Hypertension) diet is a well-rounded and flexible diet that prioritizes lowering high blood pressure and promoting overall health. This diet was developed by the National Heart, Lung, and Blood Institute (NHLBI) of the USA and encourages the consumption of nutrient-rich foods while limiting sodium, saturated fats, and added sugars. It has been extensively studied and has shown positive effects on reducing blood pressure, improving heart health, and managing weight.

The DASH diet is a whole-food style emphasizing a healthy lifestyle and physical activity. Unlike other fad diets, it is a flexible eating plan that doesn't require you to exclude any food group or reduce calories excessively. Instead, it prioritizes whole foods such as vegetables, fruits, whole grains, fat-free or low-fat dairy products, fish, poultry, beans, nuts, and vegetable oils like olive oil. These foods have been associated with improved health outcomes, including weight loss. Its flexible nature makes it easier to follow and sustain in the long run. The DASH diet promotes manageable dietary changes that are pretty flexible, and the diet plan is founded on credible nutritional advice.

Although the diet plan in question was not explicitly developed for weight loss, it is widely known that many dietary factors impacting blood pressure levels influence body weight. By adhering to this diet, you can retrain yourself to make healthier food choices. You will learn to incorporate more bulky and satiating vegetables into your meals, making them the focus of your plate and supplementing them with protein-rich foods to satisfy the meal. Additionally, you will incorporate fruits, dairy, nuts, beans, seeds, and other nutritious foods into your diet, creating a foundation for a lifetime of healthy eating habits. This approach will help you maintain healthy blood pressure levels and contribute to your overall health and well-being.

Several studies have shown that the DASH diet is an effective way to lose weight and improve health outcomes. According to one DASH study, adults who followed the DASH diet lost more weight over eight to 24 weeks than those following other low-calorie diets. Another recent survey of older adults showed that after following the DASH diet for 12 weeks, they lost an average of 6.3% body weight. In addition, blood pressure and body fat percentage decreased while all participants maintained or improved their muscle strength.

Furthermore, another small study on people with non-alcoholic liver disease found that those who followed the DASH diet for 8 weeks lost weight and improved cholesterol levels, triglyceride levels, liver enzymes, and insulin metabolism. It is believed that one of the reasons why people who follow the DASH diet lose weight and keep it off is that it is a slow and steady process. Gradually changing one's eating habits and adopting new, healthier habits helps sustain weight loss and avoid weight gain in the long run.

What is the DASH diet?

The DASH diet is a dietary approach that emphasizes consuming healthy foods, focusing on large portions of vegetables and grains. This diet recommends 3-4 ounces of lean protein like chicken, pork, seafood and more beneficial fats like olive oil. The diet encourages the intake of specific food groups, including many fruits, vegetables, whole grains, and low-fat dairy products. To promote health and reduce the risk of disease, limiting portions of higher-fat foods like red meat, fried foods, and sweets is also encouraged, as well as reducing sodium intake. It's also high in fiber, so it helps you feel full for longer. Since it also limits sweets and sugar, you are less likely to experience high blood sugar spikes when following this diet. The DASH diet plan includes nutrients known to help lower blood pressure, such as potassium, magnesium, and calcium. The DASH diet primarily focuses on improving blood pressure but can also lead to sustained weight loss as a secondary benefit.

Remember to keep in mind that the DASH Diet wasn't specifically created as a weight-loss solution. However, following this diet may lead to weight loss due to making healthier food choices. The real benefit of the DASH Diet lies in its ability to teach you healthy eating habits that you can maintain for the rest of your life. This diet can help you feel better and reduce your risk of chronic diseases by emphasizing whole, nutrient-dense foods and limiting processed and high-sugar items. So, while weight loss may be a welcome side effect, the actual value of the DASH Diet is in its ability to promote long-term health and wellness.

So, if you are looking for a diet plan that can help you shed some extra pounds while also managing your heart health and blood pressure, then the DASH diet plan could be a good option for you. This plan promotes weight loss by emphasizing whole foods, fruits, vegetables, lean proteins, and low-fat dairy products while limiting processed foods, sweets, and sugary beverages. By following this diet plan, you may be able to achieve your weight loss goals while also improving your overall health and wellness.

Features of the DASH Diet

The following charts are given out by the American Kidney Foundation on their site and pdf guide:

FOOD GROUP	DAILY SERVINGS	SERVING SIZES
Grains	6–8	1 slice bread 1 oz. dry cereal 1/2 cup cooked rice, pasta, or cereal
Vegetables	4–5	1 cup raw leafy vegetable 1/2 cup cut-up raw or cooked vegetable 1/2 cup vegetable juice
Fruits	4–5	1 medium fruit ¼ cup dried fruit 1/2 cup fresh, frozen, or canned fruit ½ cup fruit juice
Fat-free or low-fat milk and milk products	2–3	1 cup milk or yogurt 11/2 oz. cheese
Lean meats, poultry, and fish	6 or less	1 oz. cooked meats, poultry, or fish 1 egg

Nuts, seeds, and Legumes	4–5 per Week	1/3 cup or 11/2 oz. nuts 2 tbsp. peanut butter 2 tbsp. Or 1/2 oz. seeds ½ cup cooked legumes (dry beans and peas)
Fats and oils	2–3	1 tsp. soft margarine 1 tsp. vegetable oil 1 tbsp. mayonnaise 2 tbsp. salad dressing
Sweets and added Sugars	5 or fewer per week	1 tbsp. sugar 1 tbsp. jelly or jam 1/2 cup sorbet, gelatin 1 cup lemonade

Foods not allowed in the DASH diet

- ➢ Candy

- ➢ Cookies

- ➢ Chips

- ➢ Salted nuts

- ➢ Sodas

- ➢ Sugary beverages

- ➢ Pastries

- ➢ Snacks

- Meat dishes
- Prepackaged pasta and rice dishes (excluding macaroni and cheese because it is a separate category)
- Pizza
- Soups
- Salad dressings
- Cheese
- Cold cuts and cured meats
- Bread and rolls
- Sandwiches
- Sauces and gravies
- Soups

EXAMPLES OF FOODS	SOURCE OF ENERGY
Whole wheat bread and rolls, whole wheat pasta, English muffin, pita bread, bagel, cereals, grits, oatmeal, brown	Major sources of energy and fiber

rice, unsalted pretzels and popcorn	
Broccoli, carrots, collards, green beans, green peas, kale, lima beans, potatoes, spinach, squash, sweet potatoes, tomatoes	Rich sources of potassium, magnesium, and fiber
Apples, apricots, bananas, dates, grapes, oranges, grapefruit, grapefruit juice, mangoes, melons, peaches, pineapples, raisins, strawberries, tangerines	Essential sources of potassium, magnesium, and fiber
Fat-free (skim) or low-fat (1%) milk or buttermilk, fat-free, low-fat, or reduced-fat cheese, fat-free or low-fat regular or frozen yogurt	Major sources of calcium and protein
Select only lean; trim away visible fats; broil, roast, or poach; remove the skin from poultry	Rich sources of protein and Magnesium

Almonds, hazelnuts, mixed nuts, peanuts, walnuts, sunflower seeds, peanut butter, kidney beans, lentils, split peas	Rich sources of energy, magnesium, protein, and fiber
Soft margarine, vegetable oil (such as canola, corn, olive, or safflower), low-fat mayonnaise, light salad dressing	The DASH study had 27 percent of calories as fat, including fat in or added to foods
Fruit-flavored gelatin, fruit punch, hard candy, jelly, maple syrup, sorbet, and ices, sugar	Sweets should be low in fat.

Examples of SODIUM in food

Where's the Sodium?

FOOD PRODUCTS	LEVEL OF SODIUM
Whole and other grains and grain products	
Cooked cereal, rice, pasta, unsalted, 1/2 cup	0–5
Ready-to-eat cereal, 1 cup	0–360
Bread, 1 slice	110–175
Vegetables	

Fresh or frozen, cooked without salt, 1/2 cup	1–70
Canned or frozen with sauce, 1/2 cup	140–460
Tomato juice, canned, 1/2 cup	330
Fruit	
Fresh, frozen, canned, 1/2 cup	0–5
Low-fat or fat-free milk and milk products	
Milk, 1 cup	107
Yogurt, 1 cup	175
Natural cheeses, 11/2 oz.	110–450
Process cheeses, 2 oz.	600
Nuts, seeds, and legumes	
Peanuts, salted, 1/3 cup	120
Peanuts, unsalted, 1/3 cup	0–5
Beans, cooked from dried or frozen, without salt, 1/2 cup	0–5
Beans, canned, 1/2 cup	400
Lean meats, fish, and poultry	
Fresh meat, fish, poultry, 3 oz.	30–90
Tuna canned, water pack, no salt added, 3 oz.	35–45

Tuna canned, water pack, 3 oz.	230–350
Ham, lean, roasted, 3 oz.	1,020

Label Language

Food labels can benefit you by picking items lower in sodium, saturated fat, trans fat, cholesterol, and calories and higher in potassium and calcium. Search for the following label information on cans, boxes, bottles, bags, and other packaging.

Phrase	What it means
Sodium	
Sodium-free or salt-free	Less than 5 mg per serving
Very low sodium	35 mg or less of sodium per serving
Low sodium	140 mg or less of sodium per serving
Low-sodium meal	140 mg or less of sodium per 31/2 oz (100 g)
Reduced or less sodium.	At least 25 percent less sodium than the regular version

Light in sodium	50 percent less sodium than the regular version
Unsalted or no salt added.	No salt is added to the product during processing (this is not a sodium-free food)
Fat	
Fat-free	Less than 0.5 g per serving
Low saturated fat	1 g or less per serving and 15% or less of calories from saturated fat
Low-fat	3 g or less per serving
Reduced-fat	At least 25 percent less fat than the regular version
Light in fat	Half the fat compared to the regular version

Small serving sizes (50 g) or meals and main dishes are based on various weights in grams versus a serving size.

Impact on Weight Management

In addition to reducing blood pressure, the DASH diet can help with weight management and promote better heart health. The diet consists of two phases. In the first phase, you gradually decrease your saturated fat, sodium, and added sugar intake, reducing calorie and weight loss. In the second phase, you focus on healthy eating and physical activity to lose weight and lead a healthy lifestyle. Here's how the DASH diet impacts weight management:

- Nutrient-Dense Foods: The DASH diet emphasizes nutrient-rich foods that promote satiety and help control hunger, aiding in weight management.
- High in Fiber: Fiber-rich foods in the DASH diet promote feelings of fullness and reduce overall calorie intake.
- Balanced Macronutrients: The diet includes a balance of carbohydrates, protein, and healthy fats, supporting balanced energy levels and metabolism.
- Reduced Sugar and Sweets: The DASH diet helps reduce calorie intake and stabilize blood sugar levels by limiting added sugars and sweets.

Reducing sodium intake is also a vital component of the DASH diet. High-sodium diets have been linked to increased stress and adverse effects on cardiovascular health. The DASH diet supports a healthier sodium balance by focusing on lower-sodium options and using herbs and spices to flavor meals instead of excessive salt. The combination of the eating plan and a reduced sodium intake gives the most significant benefit and may help prevent the development of high blood pressure.

According to the NHLBI report, the National High Blood Pressure Education Program considers 2300mg the highest acceptable level. This is also the most elevated amount recommended for healthy Americans in the 2005 "U.S. Dietary Guidelines for Americans." To lower blood pressure further, the 1,500-milligram level is recommended by the Institute of Medicine as an adequate intake level, which most people should aim to achieve. The lower your salt intake is, the lower your blood pressure.

Therefore, **read the ingredient list carefully** for all the processed and packaged food products consumed. **Reducing salt intake requires making intelligent food choices.** Table salt and natural sodium in food contribute to a tiny portion of our overall consumption. The majority of salt and sodium in our diet comes from processed food. It's important to read food labels and select products with lower sodium content to lower your sodium intake content. You may be surprised to discover that many items, such as baked goods, certain cereals, soy sauce, seasoned salts, monosodium glutamate (MSG), baking soda, and some antacids, contain significant amounts of sodium.

Any product with more than 20% of your daily value of sodium is considered high. Low-sodium foods have ≤ less than 140 mg of sodium per serving, and very low-sodium products have ≤ less than 35 milligrams of sodium per serving. For products like canned beans and broth, choose low-sodium or no-salt-added options. Sodium lurks in unexpected places—such as salad dressings, cold cuts, bread, and cereal and therefore, you need to become an expert label reader. Sodium-free or salt-free products, on the other hand, have less than 5 mg of sodium. Lite sodium products refer to those whose sodium content has been reduced by at least 25% compared to normal ones. Finally, unsalted or no salt added means that no salt was added while processing the food.

The food ingredient label seen on most packaged and processed foods indicates the amount of sodium in each serving. It also shows whether the ingredients include salt or sodium-containing compounds, such as:

➢ Monosodium glutamate (MSG)
➢ Baking soda (also called sodium bicarbonate)
➢ Baking powder
➢ Disodium phosphate
➢ Sodium Alginate
➢ Sodium citrate
➢ Sodium nitrite

Try to dodge products with more than 200 mg of sodium per serving. Also, try to understand how many servings are in a package, as shown on the label.

Tips for easing into the DASH diet

1. Make it gradual -Start the diet by making one or two changes. Ease into the DASH diet by making minor changes to your current eating habits. Do not attempt to make many changes simultaneously, as it might cause stress and result in slip-ups, further aggravating the guilt process. This ultimately may force you to quit the diet. Break the cycle into smaller steps that are achievable to you. Even if you slip for a day or two, try to get back.

2. Increase Fruits and Vegetables: Aim to fill half your plate with various colourful fruits and vegetables at each meal.

3. Choose Whole Grains: Opt for whole grains like brown rice, quinoa, oats, and whole wheat products.

4. Limit Sodium: Be mindful of sodium content in packaged and processed foods, and use herbs and spices for flavor instead.

5. Choose Low-Fat Dairy: Opt for low-fat or fat-free dairy products to reduce saturated fat intake.

6. Snack Wisely: Choose healthy and satisfying snacks such as nuts, seeds, and fruits.

7. Choose low- or reduced-sodium, or no-salt-added versions of foods and condiments when available.

8. Choose fresh, frozen, or canned (low-sodium or no-salt-added) vegetables.

9. Include Lean Protein: Incorporate lean protein sources such as poultry, fish, beans, and tofu into your meals. When consuming meat products, go for lean cuts of meat. Always remove the skin before cooking it. Chicken, turkey, and egg are excellent options for lean cuts. Avoid processed meat products like sausage, hot dogs, and bacon. Furthermore, when buying ground meat, select those with a lower level of saturated fat. Avoid canned, smoked, or processed types.

10. Choose ready-to-eat breakfast cereals that are lower in sodium.

11. Limit cured foods (such as bacon and ham); foods packed in brine (such as pickles, pickled vegetables, olives, and sauerkraut); and condiments (such as mustard, horseradish, ketchup, and barbecue sauce).

12. Limit even lower sodium versions of soy sauce and teriyaki sauce. Treat these condiments sparingly as you do table salt.

13. Cook rice, pasta, and hot cereals without salt. Cut back on instant or flavored rice, pasta, and cereal mixes, which usually have added salt.

14. Choose "convenience" foods that are lower in sodium. Cut back on frozen dinners, mixed dishes

such as pizza, packaged mixes, canned soups or broths, and salad dressings—these often have much sodium.

15. Rinse canned foods, such as tuna and canned beans, to remove some of the sodium.

16. Use spices instead of salt. In cooking and at the table, flavor foods with herbs, spices, lemon, lime, vinegar, or salt-free seasoning blends. Start by cutting the salt in half.

17. Whenever it is possible, make your own marinades, sauces, dressings, and seasonings. Most condiments tend to be high in sodium; therefore, choose those with reduced sodium. Or go for citrus-based dressings with the same sensory taste as sodium.

18. Another essential ingredient that should be a part of the DASH diet is yogurt, especially low-fat yogurt. Yogurts are a rich source of calcium, protein, and probiotics, which can help the digestive system.

19. Encourage using oils like olive oil and rapeseed oil rather than butter, which has a higher fat content.

20. When choosing grain products, select whole-grain products rather than refined-grain products. This will help increase the fiber content of the foods, which in turn helps lower cholesterol levels.

CAUTION

It is essential to consult with a healthcare professional or a registered dietitian to personalize the DASH diet and address any specific dietary or health concerns you may have. You should be aware that the DASH eating plan has more daily servings of fruits, vegetables, and whole-grain foods than you may be used to eating. Because the plan is high in fiber, it can cause bloating and diarrhea in some persons. To avoid these problems, gradually increase your fruit, vegetables, and whole-grain foods intake.

BREAKFAST RECIPES

1. Pumpkin Pancake

These pumpkin pancakes are a nutritious and delicious way to enjoy fall flavors. The combination of pumpkin, cinnamon, and nutmeg offers a warm, comforting taste that is perfect for breakfast. Not only are these pancakes tasty, but they're also a healthy choice. Whole wheat pastry flour adds more protein, fiber, and nutrients without making them too heavy.

Pumpkin is an excellent ingredient for those following the DASH diet or trying to lose weight. It's rich in potassium, a crucial component of the DASH diet, and supports heart health by regulating blood pressure. Additionally, pumpkin is high in fiber, which helps promote a feeling of fullness and can help curb excessive calorie intake. So, if you're looking for a wholesome and satisfying breakfast option perfect for any season, especially the fall season, these pumpkin pancakes are an excellent choice.

Prep
10-15 minutes

Time
20 minutes

Service
6-8 Pencakes

Ingredients:

- 1 cup Whole Wheat Flour
- ¼ tsp. Ground Ginger
- ½ cup Oat Flour
- 2 tsp. Baking Powder
- Dash of Salt
- 1 tsp. Ground Cinnamon
- 2 Eggs, large
- ½ tsp. Ground Nutmeg
- 1 cup Pumpkin Puree
- 1 tsp. Vanilla Extract
- 1 cup Milk, low-fat

- 2 tbsp. Maple Syrup
- Cooking spray, as needed

Method of Preparation

1. Place the whole wheat flour, oat flour, baking powder, cinnamon, nutmeg, ginger, and salt in a large mixing bowl. Mix it well.

2. Whisk the pumpkin puree, milk, eggs, maple syrup, and vanilla extract in another bowl. Combine well until smooth.

3. Transfer the wet batter to the dry mixture and stir until combined. Be careful not to overmix; a few lumps are okay. Tip: Overmixing can result in dense pancakes.

4. Preheat a non-stick skillet over medium heat. Lightly grease it with cooking spray or a small amount of oil.

5. Ladle ¼ cup of batter onto the skillet for each pancake.

6. Cook for 2 to 3 minutes per side or until bubbles form on the surface and the edges look set, then turn and cook the other side until golden brown. Tip: Use a medium heat setting for the skillet to ensure even cooking without burning the pancakes.

7. Keep the cooked pancakes warm in a low oven, if needed, while using up all the batter to make the pancakes.

8. Serve the pumpkin pancakes with a dollop of Greek yogurt, a sprinkle of chopped nuts, and a drizzle of maple syrup.

Tip:

- Add spices like ground cloves or allspice to enhance the fall flavors in the pancakes.
- If the batter is too thick, you can add a little more milk. If it's too thin, add a bit more flour.
- Use any milk of your choice, such as almond milk, soy milk, or lactose-free milk, based on your dietary preferences.
- Use homemade pumpkin puree or substitute with butternut squash puree for a similar texture and flavor.

Substitution: Substitute oat flour if unavailable; you can omit it or replace it with an equal amount of whole wheat flour. Similarly, you can use buttermilk instead of low-fat milk.

Storage: The pumpkin pancakes can be stored briefly, but their texture and flavor are usually best when enjoyed fresh. To reheat refrigerated pancakes, you can use a toaster, toaster oven, or microwave. If reheating from frozen, it's best to use a toaster or toaster oven for a crispier texture. Ensure the pancakes are heated through and avoid overheating, as this may result in dry pancakes.

Nutritional Information per serving:

- ➢ **Calories:** 339Kcal
- ➢ **Carbohydrates:** 28.9g
- ➢ **Fiber:** 3.3g
- ➢ **Proteins:** 9.8g
- ➢ **Fat:** 9.7g

- ➢ **Sodium:** 90mg
- ➢ **Potassium:** 599mg
- ➢ **Calcium:** 202mg
- ➢ **Magnesium:** mg
- ➢ **Iron:** 3mg

2. Green Smoothie

Start your day off right with a refreshing green smoothie that features kale, avocado, and banana. This nutrient-packed drink is designed with the principles of the DASH Diet in mind, offering a delicious way to support your overall health and well-being. The combination of avocado, banana, and kale aligns with the DASH diet's emphasis on weight management by providing healthy monounsaturated fats, fiber, and nutrients that promote a feeling of fullness and *satiety. Avocado and kale are also rich in vitamins, antioxidants, and fiber, which help support a healthy and balanced diet. Bananas, on the other hand, offer natural sweetness and are a good source of dietary fiber, which can help reduce cravings for high-calorie snacks. This green smoothie, therefore, is a satisfying and nutritious blend that supports the DASH diet's principles of whole foods, reduced sodium, and balanced nutrient intake for effective weight management.*

Prep
5 minutes

Time
0 minutes

Service
1 Persons

Ingredients:

- 1 Banana, large & ripe
- 1 cup Baby Kale, packed, stems removed & coarsely chopped
- 1 cup Vanilla Almond Milk, unsweetened
- 2 tsp. Honey
- ¼ of 1 Avocado, ripe
- 1 cup Ice Cubes
- 1 tbsp. Chia Seeds

Method of Preparation

1. First, remove the kale leaves by slicing along each side of the stem or pulling them off, then coarsely chop the leaves.
2. Carefully cut into the avocado until the knife hits the pit.
3. First, cut the avocado lengthwise with a knife and twist the halves apart.
4. Combine banana, kale, almond milk, avocado, chia seeds, and honey in a high-speed blender.
5. Blend on high speed for 1 to 2 minutes until creamy and smooth.
6. Add ice and blend until smooth.
7. Serve and enjoy.

Tip:

- If the smoothie is too thick, add more water or almond milk until you reach your desired consistency.
- Squeeze some fresh lemon juice for brightness and a hint of acidity or sweetness to balance kale's natural bitterness.
- Avocados may oxidize and change color over time, which doesn't necessarily indicate spoilage. So, adding a bit of lemon juice to the smoothie can also minimize that.

Substitution: You can substitute baby kale with matured kale.

Storage: Green smoothies taste best when freshly made, as they help preserve their flavor and nutritional content. If you have any leftover smoothie, store it in an airtight container in the refrigerator. Consuming the leftover smoothie within 24 hours is recommended to maintain its quality in terms of taste and colour. Before drinking, make sure to shake or stir the smoothie in case any separation occurs.

Nutritional Information per serving:

- ➢ **Calories:** 343Kcal
- ➢ **Carbohydrates:** 55g
- ➢ **Fiber:** 3.3g
- ➢ **Proteins:** 6g
- ➢ **Fat:** 14g

- ➢ **Sodium:** 90mg
- ➢ **Potassium:** 599mg
- ➢ **Calcium:** 202mg
- ➢ **Magnesium:** mg
- ➢ **Iron:** 3mg

3. Breakfast Salad

Are you looking for a wholesome and nutritious breakfast option? Consider a DASH Diet-inspired breakfast salad that features egg and salsa Verde Vinaigrette. This salad is a delightful ensemble of mixed greens, hard-boiled eggs, and zesty salsa verde vinaigrette, all of which come together to create a delicious and healthy meal. The mixed greens in this salad are low in calories but high in volume, providing a sense of fullness without contributing excessive calories. Additionally, the salad is rich in dietary fiber, which enhances feelings of fullness, slows digestion, and helps regulate blood sugar levels. This can benefit weight management. The vinaigrette contains avocado and olive oil, contributing heart-healthy monounsaturated fats and adding flavor and satiety to the salad. Including healthy fats can enhance the overall satisfaction of the meal. So, if you're *looking for a tasty and nutritious way to start your day, try this breakfast salad and enjoy its fantastic taste and health benefits.*

Prep
10 minutes

Time
1-2 minutes

Service
1 Persons

Ingredients:

- 1 Egg, large
- 2 cups Mixed Salad Greens
- 3 tbsp. Salsa Verde
- 1 tbsp. + 1 tsp. Extra-Virgin Olive Oil, divided
- 2 tbsp. Cilantro, chopped plus more for garnish
- 1 Egg, large
- 1 tbsp. Pumpkin Seeds
- ½ cup Red Kidney Beans, low-sodium & washed
- ¼ of 1 Avocado, sliced

Method of Preparation

1. Whisk salsa, 1 tbsp. oil, and cilantro in a small bowl.
2. Toss half the salsa mixture with salad greens in a shallow dinner bowl.
3. Assemble beans and avocado in a layer atop the salad.

4. Take a small nonstick skillet and heat it over medium-high heat.
5. Once hot, spoon in the remaining 1 tsp. oil.
6. Add the egg and fry for 1 to 2 minutes or until the white is thoroughly cooked but the yolk is still slightly runny.
7. Serve the egg on the salad. Drizzle with the remaining salsa vinaigrette. Tip: Toss the salad gently to ensure an even vinaigrette coating.
8. Sprinkle the pumpkin seeds on top for extra crunch.

Tip:

- Enhance the flavor of the vinaigrette by adding fresh herbs like cilantro or parsley.
- Feel free to add vegetables like radishes or red onion for flavor and nutrition.
- You can top the salad with sliced strawberries, blueberries, or a handful of whole-grain croutons for extra taste, texture, and nutrition.

Substitution: Use any leafy greens, such as romaine lettuce, kale, or mixed baby greens.

Storage: Enjoy the breakfast salad immediately for optimal freshness. Consume within 24 hours for best quality. Fresh veggies lose flavor and texture over time. Separate dressing and components to maintain freshness.

Nutritional Information per serving:

- ➢ **Calories**: 527Kcal
- ➢ **Carbohydrates**: 37g
- ➢ **Fiber**: 13g
- ➢ **Proteins**: 16g
- ➢ **Fat**: 34g

- ➢ **Sodium**: 228mg
- ➢ **Potassium**: 1001mg
- ➢ **Calcium**: 182mg
- ➢ **Magnesium**: mg
- ➢ **Iron**:7mg

4. White Bean Avocado Toast

This delectable white bean and avocado toast is a savory and satisfying dish crafted in harmony with the principles of the DASH diet. This wholesome recipe combines the creamy richness of ripe avocado, the heart-healthy goodness of white beans, and the fiber-packed embrace of whole-grain bread. Each bite celebrates flavor and nutrition, embodying the DASH diet's commitment to nourishing the body while supporting overall well-being.

Furthermore, avocados and white beans are nutrient-dense foods, providing a variety of essential vitamins, minerals, and antioxidants. Consuming nutrient-dense foods supports overall health and helps meet nutritional needs without *excess calories. On top, the combination of carbohydrates from the bread, healthy fats from avocado and olive oil, and protein from white beans creates a well-balanced meal that supports sustained energy levels and helps control appetite.*

Prep
5-10 minutes

Time
1-2 minutes

Service
1 Persons

Ingredients:

- 1 slice of Whole-Wheat Bread, toasted
- ½ cup White Beans, rinsed and drained
- ¼ of 1 Avocado, ripe & mashed
- 1 tsp. Lemon Juice
- Ground Pepper, as needed
- 1 tsp. Extra Virgin Olive Oil
- 1 pinch Crushed Red Pepper

Method of Preparation

1. Please toast the slice of whole-grain bread to your desired level of crispiness.
2. Mash the ripe avocado in a bowl with a fork. Add a pinch of salt, pepper, and half lemon juice. Combine well. Tip: Lemon juice adds a zesty flavor and

provides acidity, enhancing the overall taste. Adjust to taste.

3. Place the white beans, remaining lemon juice, extra-virgin olive oil, salt, and pepper in another bowl. Mash the beans slightly with a fork to create a chunky mixture.

4. Spread mashed avocado and white beans on toast. Season with salt, pepper, and crushed red pepper.

5. Serve and enjoy.

Tip:

- Garnish with optional toppings such as halved cherry tomatoes, red pepper flakes, or fresh herbs to enhance both flavor and presentation.

- Add a source of lean protein, such as grilled chicken or smoked salmon, to increase the protein content of the toast.

- Fresh herbs like parsley, chives, or cilantro can enhance the flavor of the toast without adding salt.

- For a unique twist, drizzle a small amount of almond or cashew butter on top.

- It is best to prepare the avocado and white bean mixture just before assembling the toast to prevent it from getting soggy and to maintain its freshness.

Substitution: If you don't like avocado, try substituting it with hummus, mashed peas, or a small amount of guacamole for a similar creamy texture.

Storage: Freshly made Avocado toast tastes best to preserve its texture and flavors. If you have mixed the avocado with lemon juice and want to store it separately, place it in an airtight container and refrigerate it for a short duration, preferably no longer than 24 hours.

However, if you want to prepare the bread in advance, cool it completely and store it in a paper bag at room temperature. Toasted bread tends to lose its crispness when stored, so it's best to reheat it briefly in a toaster before assembling the toast.

Please remember that the toast's quality, especially the bread's crispiness, may diminish when refrigerated. Therefore, it is recommended to consume the toast shortly after it is prepared to enjoy the best flavors.

Nutritional Information per serving:

- ➢ **Calories:** 230
- ➢ **Carbohydrates**: 35g
- ➢ **Fiber**: 11g
- ➢ **Proteins:** 12g
- ➢ **Fat**:9g

- ➢ **Sodium**: 400mg
- ➢ **Potassium:** 655mg
- ➢ **Calcium:** 93mg
- ➢ **Magnesium:** 93mg
- ➢ **Iron**:2mg

5. Overnight Oats

Start your day with a nourishing and delicious breakfast that prioritizes your health and satisfies your taste buds. The DASH diet emphasizes whole foods and vibrant flavors, making it a culinary pleasure. This overnight oat recipe is a simple and convenient way to prepare breakfast the night before. Soaking oats and chia seeds in almond milk creates a creamy and satisfying texture that is perfect for a busy morning.

Berries, chia seeds, and almond milk are all nutrient-dense foods that provide essential vitamins, minerals, and antioxidants. These foods can help you meet your nutritional needs while managing your calorie intake, which is necessary for effective and sustainable weight loss. Chia seeds are especially beneficial because they contain fiber, omega-3 fatty acids, and protein. The soluble fiber in chia seeds *absorbs water, creating a gel-like consistency that can help you feel full and satisfied. The healthy fats in almond milk provide satiety, and protein is essential for maintaining muscle mass during weight loss.*

Prep
5-10 minutes

Time
0 minutes

Service
1-2 Persons

Ingredients:

- 1 Banana, mashed
- ½ cup Rolled Oats
- 2 tbsp. Blackberries
- 2 tbsp. Chia Seeds
- ¼ tsp. Vanilla Extract
- ½ cup Almond Milk
- 2 tbsp. Blueberries
- ¼ cup Water
- ¼ tsp. Ground Cinnamon

Method of Preparation:

1. To begin with, place the rolled oats and chia seeds in an airtight container or jar.
2. Next, pour almond milk into it and spoon in vanilla extract. Stir well to ensure the oats and chia seeds are fully submerged in the liquid.
3. Then, stir in all the remaining ingredients, excluding the berries, and gently mix until everything comes together.
4. Cover the container with a lid and refrigerate for at least 4-6 hours. This allows the oats and chia seeds to absorb the liquid and soften.
5. In the morning, gently fold in the berries. Enjoy.
6. Sprinkle sliced almonds on top for added crunch and nutrition.

Tip:

- For a fiber-rich base, choose rolled or old-fashioned oats over instant oats that may contain added sugars and lower fiber content.
- If the consistency is too thick, add more almond milk until it reaches your desired thickness.
- Personalize your bowl of oats by adding toppings such as sliced almonds, flaxseeds, or Greek yogurt for extra protein.

- For a creamy and nutty taste, add a tablespoon of almond butter, peanut butter, or cashew butter and swirl.
- For added texture and sweetness, consider including small amounts of dried fruit such as raisins, cranberries, or chopped dates.
- For an extra protein boost, add a scoop of your favorite protein powder or a dollop of Greek yogurt.
- Add a dash of nutmeg or cardamom for extra flavor, in addition to or in place of cinnamon.

Substitution: You can choose any plant-based milk alternative, like soy, oat, or coconut milk. Make sure that it is unsweetened to follow the principles of the DASH diet. Also, if you don't have chia seeds, you can use flaxseeds or hemp seeds to add texture and nutrition to your diet.

Storage: Overnight oats prepared with chia seeds, berries, and almond milk should be consumed within 4 to 6 hours of preparation to maintain their optimal texture and freshness. This ensures that the oats remain chewy and don't become too soft. You can store the oats in an airtight container in the refrigerator for up to 2-3 days. However, the texture of the oats may change over time as the oats and chia seeds continue to absorb liquid.

Nutritional Information per serving:

- ➤ **Calories:** 246Kcal
- ➤ **Carbohydrates**: 44g
- ➤ **Fiber**: 13g
- ➤ **Proteins:** 6.5g
- ➤ **Fat:** 6g

- ➤ **Sodium**: 228mg
- ➤ **Potassium:** 1001mg
- ➤ **Calcium:** 182mg
- ➤ **Magnesium:** mg
- ➤ **Iron:**7mg

6. Mango Ginger Smoothie

The Mango Ginger Smoothie with Red Lentils is a well-crafted, nutritious beverage that considers the principles of the DASH diet. With its vibrant color and taste, this smoothie is rich in fruits, vegetables, and low-fat dairy, making it an ideal choice for those who want to follow the DASH diet. It also features red lentils, an excellent source of protein and fiber, contributing to the smoothie's overall health benefits.

The smoothie's natural sweetness comes from the mango, which pairs perfectly with the fresh ginger's zesty kick, creating a flavor combination that is both bold and refreshing. Additionally, the red lentils add plant-based protein while also adding to the smoothie's satiety and heart-healthy components. Compared to nonfat plain yogurt, the lentils add 3 grams more protein per equal-sized portion, and *compared to protein powder, they add 4 grams more fiber per serving.*

So, if you're looking for a tasty and health-conscious option, the mango ginger smoothie with red lentils is an excellent choice. This smoothie is packed with vitamins, minerals, and dietary fiber, making it an excellent way to support your cardiovascular health while tantalizing your taste buds with its tropical and refreshing blend.

Prep
10 minutes

Time
0 minutes

Service
1 Persons

Ingredients:

- ½ cup Red Lentils, cooked & cooled
- ¾ cup Carrot Juice
- 1 tbsp. Chia Seeds
- 1 cup Mango Chunks, frozen
- 1 tsp. Honey
- 1 tsp. Ginger, fresh & chopped
- Pinch of ground Cardamom + more for garnish
- ¼ cup Greek Yogurt
- 3 Ice Cubes

Method of Preparation:

1. Place cooked lentils, mango, carrot juice, ginger, honey, cardamom, and ice cubes in a high-speed blender.
2. Blend on high speed for 2 to 3 minutes or until smooth and creamy.
3. Garnish with more cardamom, if desired.

Tips:

- To cook lentils, start by washing red ones thoroughly and then boiling them for about 15 minutes or until they are tender. Once cooked, drain the lentils and allow them to cool completely, ensuring a smooth texture. Remember that 1 cup of dry lentils yields 2 ½ cups of cooked lentils. You can store cooked lentils in the refrigerator for up to 3 days.
- If the smoothie is too thick, add more water or almond milk and blend until you reach your desired consistency.
- Add other nutritious additions, such as spinach or kale, to boost the smoothie's nutrient content.

Substitution: Instead of red lentils, you can use green lentils, brown lentils, or yellow lentils. Similarly, you can use frozen fruits like frozen peach or pineapple that are naturally sweet to maintain the flavor profile.

Storage: For the best taste and maximum nutrients, consuming your smoothie immediately after preparing it is recommended. If you need to store it, refrigerate it in an airtight container. However, if you are storing your smoothie in the fridge, consume it within 24 hours to ensure it retains its optimal taste and nutrients. Before drinking a refrigerated or thawed smoothie, shake or blend it to restore its consistency.

Nutritional Information per serving:

- **Calories**: 352Kcal
- **Fat**: 9.8g
- **Carbohydrates**: 23.1g
- **Fiber**: 10g
- **Proteins**: 12g

- **Sodium:** 122mg
- **Potassium:** 787mg
- **Magnesium:** 49mg
- **Calcium:** 64mg
- **Iron:** 4mg

7. Grain & Dried Fruits Salad

Indulge in a wholesome and heart-healthy morning delight with this exquisite grain and dried fruit salad. Carefully crafted with the principles of the DASH diet, this nutritious breakfast bowl is a perfect combination of whole grains, vibrant fruits, and creamy yogurt that supports cardiovascular health and overall well-being.

Savor the exquisite blend of sweet and crisp apples with the creamy richness of low-fat vanilla yogurt, all nestled on a bed of quick-cooking brown rice and bulgur. The fresh oranges and plump raisins elevate the dish, offering a burst of natural sweetness and a medley of textures to delight your palate.

This breakfast bowl is perfect for those who prioritize nutrient-dense and heart-smart ingredients. So, whether you're seeking a satisfying start to your day or exploring a breakfast option that balances flavor and nutrition, this fare is the perfect choice that caters to your taste buds and well-being.

Prep
10 minutes

Time
10-15 minutes

Service
2 Persons

Ingredients:

- 1 Red Delicious Apple
- 3 cups Water
- 8 oz. low-fat Vanilla Yogurt
- Pinch of Salt
- 1 Orange
- ¾ cup quick-cooking Brown Rice
- ¾ cup Bulgur
- 1 Granny Smith Apple
- 1 cup Raisins

Method of Preparation:

1. Heat water and salt in a large pot to boil over high heat.

2. Stir in rice and bulgur into it. Lower the heat to low, and cook for 10 minutes while covering it.

3. Remove from heat and keep it aside, covered for 2 minutes.

4. Spread the hot grains on a baking sheet to cool them. Grains can be prepared the night before and kept in the refrigerator.

5. Before serving, prepare the fruit by coring and chopping the apples. Peel the orange and cut it into sections.

6. Transfer the chilled grains and cut fruit to a medium mixing bowl. Spoon in the yogurt into the grains and fruit until coated.

7. Serve and enjoy.

Tips:

- If you find that the natural sweetness from the fruits and raisins in your yogurt is insufficient, you may add a small amount of honey or maple syrup.

- Additionally, you can add other ingredients, such as seeds, coconut flakes, or spices, to enhance the flavor.

Substitution: The recipe suggests using Fuji, Gala, or Honeycrisp apples as a substitute for Granny Smith apples. Additionally, quinoa or couscous can be used instead of bulgur.

Storage: This fare salad can be stored in the refrigerator in an airtight container for 2 to 3 days. Store the individual components separately to maintain their freshness and prevent sogginess if possible.

Nutritional Information per serving:

- ➤ **Calories:** 197Kcal
- ➤ **Fat:** 9.8g
- ➤ **Saturated Fat:** 3.5g
- ➤ **Carbohydrates:** 23.1g
- ➤ **Fiber:** 3.6g

- ➤ **Sodium:** 96mg
- ➤ **Potassium:** 319mg
- ➤ **Calcium:** 28mg
- ➤ **Iron:** 3mg
- ➤ **Proteins:** 6.2g

8. Quinoa Oatmeal

The Quinoa oatmeal breakfast bowl is a nutritious and tasty combination of two superfoods - quinoa and oats - that make for a hearty and heart-healthy start to your day. This wholesome creation is packed with essential nutrients, protein, and fiber that nourish your body and keep you feeling full and energized. The addition of cinnamon and vanilla not only infuses warmth and sweetness but also adds to the nutritional value of the dish.

Moreover, the recipe is highly customizable, allowing you to swap in your preferred nuts, fruits, or sweeteners based on your dietary preferences and needs. Whether you are looking for a delicious and satisfying breakfast or a wholesome meal to support your well-being, the quinoa oatmeal breakfast bowl is perfect. So, go ahead and indulge *in this delightful and nutritious breakfast dish that promises to leave you feeling nourished and satisfied all morning long. Alongside, the quinoa oatmeal recipe benefits weight loss due to its combination of quinoa and oats, providing a satisfying blend of protein and fiber that promotes feelings of fullness.*

Prep
10 minutes

Time
20-25 minutes

Service
2 Persons

Ingredients:

- 2 cups low-fat Milk
- ½ cup Old-fashioned Rolled Oats
- ¼ cup Honey
- ½ cup Quinoa, uncooked
- ¼ tsp. Vanilla Extract
- ¼ cup Almonds, slivered
- ¼ tsp. Ground Cinnamon + more to taste
- ¼ cup Dried Currants, chopped dried apricots

Method of Preparation:

1. Wash the quinoa thoroughly. You can rinse using a fine-mesh sieve to remove the residual bitterness.

2. Pour the milk into a medium saucepan and boil. Once it starts boiling, stir in the quinoa and return to a boil. Tip: Ensure the proper liquid ratio to grains to achieve the desired consistency. You can adjust as needed during cooking.

3. Cover the pan with a lid and lower the heat to medium-low. Allow it to simmer for 12 to 15 minutes or until most liquid is absorbed.

4. Take the pan off the heat and fluff the cooked quinoa with a fork.

5. Add the remaining ingredients, cover, and set it aside for 15 minutes.

6. Top with fresh berries or sliced fruit, and garnish with more chopped nuts or seeds if desired.

Tips:

- You can add flavorings like nutmeg, cardamom, or a dash of citrus zest for variety.

Substitution: You can use bulgur, farro, or amaranth instead of quinoa.

Storage: It is recommended to consume quinoa oatmeal freshly prepared to enjoy its optimal taste and texture. However, if you want to store it, you can do so in an airtight container in the refrigerator for 2 to 3 days. When reheating, add a splash of milk or water to restore moisture and creaminess. Warm it up in the microwave or on the stovetop until it's heated through.

Nutritional Information per serving:

- ➢ **Calories:** 340Kcal
- ➢ **Fat:** 9.3g
- ➢ **Carbohydrates:** 51.8g
- ➢ **Fiber:** 5.7g
- ➢ **Proteins:** 13.2g

- ➢ **Sodium:** 96mg
- ➢ **Potassium:** 555mg
- ➢ **Magnesium:** 34mg
- ➢ **Calcium:** 188mg
- ➢ **Iron:** 3mg

9. Greek Yogurt Parfait

The Greek Yogurt Parfait is a nutritious and delectable treat that incorporates the creamy texture of Greek yogurt, the freshness of clementines, and the crunch of granola. This delightful dessert features layers of non-fat Greek yogurt that are rich in protein, a blend of antioxidant-packed pistachios and clementines, and a sprinkle of low-sugar, whole-grain granola for added texture and satisfaction. This versatile parfait can be enjoyed as a fulfilling breakfast, refreshing snack, or healthy dessert.

Each layer of the Greek yogurt parfait contains nutrition that promotes a heart-healthy lifestyle and a delightful culinary experience. Additionally, this parfait is an excellent option for those looking to lose weight, as it contains non-fat Greek yogurt that encourages satiety and fresh clementines that add

*natural sweetness and essential vitamins without adding
excessive calories. The measured serving of low-sugar
granola provides satisfying crunch and whole-grain benefits,
making this parfait a healthy, balanced alternative for those
seeking weight management through nutritious, portion-
controlled meals.*

Prep
10 minutes

Time
0 minutes

Service
1 Persons

Ingredients:

- ¼ cup shelled Pistachios, unsalted, dry-roasted & chopped
- 2 tbsp. Granola
- 3 cups plain fat-free Greek-Style Yogurt
- 4 tsp. Honey
- 1 tsp. Vanilla Extract
- 28 Clementine Segments

Method of Preparation:

1. Place yogurt and vanilla extract in a medium bowl. Mix well.
2. Spoon 1/3 cup of the yogurt mixture into each of 4 small parfait glasses. Top each with 5 clementine

sections, ½ tbsp. of nuts, ½ tbsp. of granola and ½ tsp. of honey.

3. Top each parfait with the remaining yogurt mixture (about 1/3 cup). Add 2 clementine segments, ½ tbsp. nuts, and ½ tsp. honey on top of each parfait.

4. Serve immediately.

Tip: Experiment with different layering options, such as alternating yogurt and berries or creating artistic patterns for visual appeal.

Substitution: Instead of Greek yogurt, you can use regular yogurt (choose low-fat or non-fat for a lighter option), or plant-based yogurt (almond, coconut, soy) for a dairy-free alternative.

Storage: The Greek yogurt parfait is best consumed immediately after assembling to maintain its texture and freshness. If you need to store it, place the parfait in an airtight container, cover it tightly with plastic wrap, and keep it in the refrigerator for 1 to 2 days. It's essential to remember that the longer the parfait sits, the more likely it is for the granola to lose its crunch, and the fruits may release juices, which could affect the texture. Therefore, if you're making it ahead of time, it's often best to prepare the components separately and combine them just before serving.

Nutritional Information per serving:

- ➢ **Calories:** 312Kcal
- ➢ **Fat:** 27.1gm
- ➢ **Carbohydrates:** 81.7g
- ➢ **Fiber:** 11g
- ➢ **Proteins:** 29.2g

- ➢ **Sodium:** 109mg
- ➢ **Potassium:** 953mg
- ➢ **Magnesium:** 24mg
- ➢ **Calcium:** 419mg
- ➢ **Iron:** 5mg

10. Herbed Omelette

Here is a nutritious and flavorful dish that elevates the classic omelet with the vibrant goodness of fresh herbs and the wholesome crunch of finely chopped broccoli—the Herbed Broccoli Omelet. On top, this delightful creation effortlessly combines protein-packed eggs with nutrient-dense vegetables, offering a balanced and heart-healthy breakfast for two.

This omelet is a symphony of colors and textures, featuring the verdant hues of finely chopped broccoli, the aromatic essence of fresh herbs, and the sweetness of diced red bell peppers and onions. A touch of optional low-fat feta cheese adds a savory element. Whether you're seeking a satisfying breakfast or a light brunch option, the Herbed Broccoli Omelet is a wholesome choice that embodies both nutritional excellence and culinary delight.

Prep
10-15 minutes

Time
10-12 minutes

Service
2 Persons

Ingredients:

- 4 Eggs
- Dash of Salt
- 1 cup Broccoli, chopped
- ¼ cup Onion, finely diced
- ¼ tsp Dried Marjoram
- ⅛ tsp Pepper
- 1 tbsp. Olive Oil
- ¼ cup Red Bell Pepper, finely diced
- 1 tbsp. Parsley, fresh & chopped
- 2 tbsp. Feta Cheese, low-fat, low-salt & crumbled

Method of Preparation:

1. Whisk eggs with salt, marjoram, and pepper in a medium bowl.
2. Heat oil in a large skillet on medium- high heat.
3. Stir onion, bell pepper, and broccoli into it.
4. Cook for 4 to 5 minutes or until the vegetables are tender crisp. Add pepper as needed.

5. Pour the whisked eggs over the sautéed vegetables and then sprinkle the low-fat cheese over one-half of the omelet. Tip: Cook the eggs over low to medium heat to prevent overcooking and ensure a moist omelet.

6. Cook until nearly set, lifting up cooked edges to let uncooked egg flow underneath. At this point, the omelet should be completely set but still moist in the center.

7. Flip the omelet; cook. Halve and divide between 2 plates.

8. Garnish it with parsley. Omelets are best enjoyed fresh and hot, so serve immediately after cooking.

Tips:

- You can add fresh herbs like parsley, chives, or cilantro for added freshness and flavor.
- Pair the omelet with whole-grain toast or a side of fruit for a well-balanced meal.

Substitution: You can substitute broccoli with cauliflower, asparagus, spinach, kale, or any preferred vegetables.

Storage: Store the leftover omelet in an airtight container in the refrigerator for 1 to 2 days. Reheat gently in a pan or microwave, adding a splash of water to retain moisture. The texture of vegetables and eggs may change upon refrigeration, so be aware that the reheated omelet may not have the same texture as when freshly cooked. When reheating, use low to medium heat to prevent overcooking and maintain moisture. Consider adding fresh herbs or a sprinkle of cheese after reheating for added flavor.

Nutritional Information per serving:

- ➢ **Calories:** 251Kcal
- ➢ **Fat:** 18g
- ➢ **Carbohydrates:** 9.9g
- ➢ **Fiber:** 3.5g
- ➢ **Proteins:** 15.3g

- ➢ **Sodium:** 96mg
- ➢ **Potassium:** 610mg
- ➢ **Calcium:** 194mg
- ➢ **Iron:** 5mg

LUNCH RECIPES

1. Brussels Sprout with Lemon Herb Tilapia

If you're looking for a delicious and heart-healthy meal, you might want to try the Brussels Sprouts and Lemon Herb Tilapia recipe. This dish is not only delicious but also in line with the principles of the DASH diet, making it an excellent option for those who want to maintain a balanced and nutritious diet. It features light and flaky tilapia, tender Brussels sprouts, and an assortment of colorful vegetables. On top of that, it provides a wholesome and satisfying meal catering to taste and well-being.

Moreover, Brussels sprouts are an excellent choice for weight loss, thanks to their low-calorie content and high fiber, which can help control appetite and promote a sense of *fullness. These cruciferous vegetables are nutrient-dense, offering essential vitamins and minerals crucial for overall well-being without adding unnecessary calories. Their satisfying texture, nutritional richness, and metabolism-supporting properties make Brussels sprouts a nutritious and flavorful addition to a weight-conscious diet.*

Prep
15 minutes

Time
20 minutes

Service
4 Persons

Ingredients:

- 4 Tilapia Fillets
- 2 tbsp. Olive Oil
- 1 lb. Brussels Sprouts, trimmed & halved
- 3 cloves Garlic, minced
- 1 tsp. Rosemary, fresh & chopped
- 1 cup Cherry Tomatoes, halved
- 1 tsp. Thyme, fresh & chopped
- Zest of 1 Lemon
- ¼ cup Parsley for garnish, chopped fresh
- Juice of 1 Lemon
- Dash of Salt and Pepper
- Cooked Quinoa or Brown Rice for serving

Method of Preparation:

1. Steam the Brussels sprouts in a steamer for 3-4 minutes or until they are slightly tender but still vibrant green. Keep it aside.

2. Marinate the tilapia fillets with salt, pepper, and half of the minced garlic.

3. Heat 1 tablespoon of olive oil over medium-high heat in a large skillet.

4. Once hot, place the tilapia fillets in it and cook on each side for 3-4 minutes or until the fish flakes easily with a fork. Remove tilapia from the skillet and keep it aside.

5. Spoon another tablespoon of olive oil into the same skillet.

6. Stir in the remaining minced garlic, chopped thyme, and rosemary.

7. Cook for about 30 seconds or until aromatic.

8. Add the halved Brussels sprouts and cherry tomatoes. Sauté them for 4-5 minutes or until the vegetables are tender-crisp.

9. Return the cooked tilapia fillets to the skillet with the vegetables.

10. Sprinkle lemon zest and juice over fish and veggies. Toss gently.

11. Garnish the dish with chopped fresh parsley, if desired, and serve it over cooked quinoa or brown rice.

Tip:

- If you prefer a touch of sweetness but want to avoid honey or maple syrup, try using agave nectar or a sugar substitute.
- Add a crunchy texture by incorporating toasted almonds, sesame seeds, or sunflower seeds.

Substitution: Feel free to substitute Brussels sprouts with other cruciferous vegetables like broccoli or cauliflower. Similarly, Replace tilapia with other lean proteins like chicken breast, turkey, tofu, or tempeh.

Storage: This fare can be stored in the refrigerator in an airtight container for 3 to 4 days. When reheating, ensure the dish reaches an internal temperature of 165°F (74°C) to ensure food safety. Reheat in the microwave or on the stovetop until thoroughly heated.

Nutritional Information per serving:

- **Calories:** 256Kcal
- **Fat:** 8.8g
- **Carbohydrates:** 23.9g
- **Fiber:** 2.6g
- **Proteins:** 21.9g

- **Sodium:** 48mg
- **Potassium:** 273mg
- **Magnesium:** 69mg
- **Calcium:** 58mg
- **Iron:** 3mg

2. Vegetable Mulligatawny Soup

This hearty soup is crafted to tantalize your taste buds and promote heart health and weight management through thoughtfully selected ingredients and mindful preparation. From the fiber-packed red lentils to the abundance of leafy greens and aromatic spices, every ingredient is designed to nourish your body while adhering to the DASH diet's recommendations. Furthermore, the low-sodium vegetable broth ensures sodium intake remains within the recommended limits while fostering a diet prioritizing cardiovascular health. On top, the soup has spinach, which is packed with potassium, magnesium, and fiber; spinach supports blood pressure management and promotes heart health—a cornerstone of the DASH diet. Furthermore, its low-calorie density and high fiber content increase feelings *of fullness, making it an excellent choice for weight loss by aiding in calorie control.*

Prep
15 minutes

Time
50 minutes

Service
4 Persons

Ingredients:

- 3 tbsp. Extra-Virgin Olive Oil, divided
- 1 tbsp. Curry Powder
- 1 Onion, medium & chopped finely
- 2 Carrots, medium & finely chopped
- ½ cup Spinach, chopped
- 1 Green Apple, medium, peeled & finely chopped
- 1 Parsnip, medium, peeled & finely chopped
- 4 cups diced Acorn Squash, peeled
- 4 cups Vegetable Broth, low-sodium
- 3 cloves Garlic, minced, divided
- 1 tsp. fresh Ginger, grated
- 1 ×14 oz. can No-Salt-Added Diced Tomatoes
- ½ cup Red Lentils, washed & drained
- ¼ cup Cilantro, fresh & chopped, plus more for garnish
- 2 whole-wheat naan flatbreads, halved

Method of Preparation:

1. Preheat the oven to 190° C or 375°F. Line a baking sheet with foil.
2. Heat a large saucepan over medium heat, and spoon in the oil once hot.
3. Once it starts simmering, stir in the onion, carrots, parsnip, and sauté them for 6 minutes or until the onions are translucent.
4. Add squash, apple, curry powder, 2 cloves garlic, and ginger and cook for 1 to 2 minutes while stirring, until aromatic.
5. Next, pour the broth, tomatoes, and lentils and mix well.
6. Bring the mixture to a boil. Lower the heat and allow it to simmer while keeping it covered.
7. Cook for 18 to 20 minutes or until the squash and lentils are tender.
8. Stir in the spinach and cook for 5 minutes or until the greens are wilted. Tip: Adding spinach at the end will retain its vibrant color and nutritional value.
9. In the meantime, apply one side of each naan with the remaining 1 tablespoon of oil.
10. Top it with the remaining 1 minced garlic clove and keep it on the prepared baking sheet.
11. Bake for 5 to 6 minutes or until warm. Remove from oven and sprinkle with cilantro.

12. Transfer half of the soup to a blender and puree. Garnish the soup with cilantro and serve with the naan.
13. Serve and enjoy.

Tip:

- If you like chunky soup, gently mash it with a potato masher rather than blending half of it in the blender.
- To make the soup more nutritious and filling, you can add brown rice or quinoa to the soup.

Substitution: Instead of acorn squash, you can use butternut squash. If you don't have curry powder, you can blend ground cumin, coriander, turmeric, and a pinch of cinnamon to create a similar flavor profile.

Storage: The soup fare will stay suitable for up to 4 days when stored in airtight containers in the refrigerator. Reheat gently on the stove, adding a splash of water if needed to maintain the soup's consistency.

Nutritional Information per serving:

- ➤ **Calories:** 487Kcal
- ➤ **Carbohydrates**: 76g
- ➤ **Proteins:** 14g
- ➤ **Fat:** 15g
- ➤ **Proteins:** 21.9g

- ➤ **Sodium**: 406mg
- ➤ **Potassium:** 1044mg
- ➤ **Calcium:** 159mg
- ➤ **Magnesium:** 90mg
- ➤ **Iron:** 5mg

3. Shrimp with Vegetables

Indulge in the delectable taste of barbecue-glazed shrimp that not only gratifies your taste buds but also adheres to the principles of the DASH diet. The medley of colourful bell peppers, juicy cherry tomatoes, and tender zucchini infuses a burst of flavor. At the same time, the plethora of vitamins, minerals, and antioxidants in these veggies enhances the dish's nutritional value. Accompanied by whole-grain orzo, this meal provides a perfectly balanced serving of whole foods, lean proteins, and heart-healthy fats that align with the DASH diet's recommendations. As you savor each succulent bite, delight in knowing that this barbecue-glazed shrimp fare is delicious and nourishing, promoting a heart-conscious and wholesome eating pattern.

Shrimp, a prime source of protein, is also low in saturated fat and calories, making it an ideal food choice for people following the DASH diet. When paired with zucchini, a nutrient-dense and low-calorie vegetable, this combination provides a delectable and satiating option for weight management. Together, they form a perfect blend of essential nutrients that fuel your body and promote a balanced, heart-healthy eating pattern.

Prep
15 minutes

Time
30 minutes

Service
4 Persons

Ingredients:

- 1 lb. Jumbo Shrimp, peeled & deveined
- 2 cups Zucchini, coarsely chopped
- 1 tsp. Paprika
- 1 cup Whole-Grain Orzo
- ½ tsp. Garlic Powder
- ½ cup Celery, thinly sliced
- ½ tsp. dried Oregano, crushed
- 1 cup Bell Pepper, coarsely chopped
- ¼ tsp. ground Pepper
- 2 tbsp. Barbecue Sauce, low-sodium
- ⅛ tsp. Cayenne Pepper
- 3 Scallions, sliced, white & green parts separated

- 2 tbsp. Olive oil, divided
- 1 cup Cherry Tomatoes, halved
- Pinch of Salt
- Lemon wedges for serving

Method of Preparation:

1. To start with, keep the shrimp in a medium-sized bowl.

2. Mix paprika, garlic powder, oregano, pepper, and cayenne in another small bowl. Spoon in the spice mixture over the shrimp. Coat it well.

3. Heat a large saucepan of water to a boil over medium heat. Cook the orzo by following the package directions. Once cooked, drain it well. Return the pasta to the hot pot; cover and keep warm.

4. Heat a medium-sized skillet over medium-high heat. Pour oil and stir in the scallion whites, zucchini, bell pepper, and celery; sauté for 10 to 15 minutes, stirring occasionally, until the vegetables are crisp-tender.

5. Add tomatoes; cook 2 to 3 minutes more until softened. Add the vegetables to the pot with the orzo. Spoon in the salt and mix well.

6. Heat the remaining oil over medium heat in the same skillet. Add the shrimp; cook for 4 to 6 minutes while turning once, until the shrimp is pink and opaque. Pour the barbecue sauce. Cook for another 1 minute and stir until the shrimp are coated. Tip: Be cautious

not to overcook the shrimp. Shrimp cook quickly, and overcooking can result in a rubbery texture.

7. Serve the shrimp and vegetable mixture with scallion greens and lemon wedges.

Tip:

1. If desired, garnish it with freshly chopped parsley for a burst of freshness.
2. Adjust the amount of grated ginger, or add red pepper flakes if you enjoy a bit of heat.

Substitution: Substitute shrimp with grilled chicken breast strips, tofu cubes, or white fish fillets for a different protein source.

Storage: The fare will stay suitable for up to 4 days when stored in airtight containers in the refrigerator. When reheating leftovers, sprinkle a little water over the orzo before microwaving to prevent it from drying out.

Nutritional Information per serving:

➢ **Calories:** 360Kcal

➢ **Carbohydrates:** 41g

➢ **Fiber:** 10g

➢ **Proteins:** 30g

➢ **Fat:** 9g

➢ **Sodium:** 554mg

➢ **Potassium:** 734mg

➢ **Calcium:** 109mg

➢ **Magnesium:** 66mg

➢ **Iron:**2mg

4. Cauliflower & Broccoli Soup

This simple yet satisfying soup recipe combines the goodness of cauliflower and broccoli, creating a wholesome dish that not only tantalizes your taste buds but also aligns with your health goals. Cauliflower and broccoli are low in calories but high in essential nutrients, making them ideal companions for a weight loss-focused menu. Packed with fiber, they contribute to a feeling of fullness, curbing those between-meal cravings and promoting satiety. Furthermore, their low energy density, coupled with a wealth of vitamins, minerals,

and antioxidants, underscores their significance in a balanced diet aimed at shedding excess weight while promoting overall cardiovascular health. Rich in fiber, low in calories, and with a minimal impact on blood sugar levels, these vegetables form a cornerstone of the DASH diet's focus on reducing sodium intake while maximizing nutritional content.

Prep
15 minutes

Time
45 minutes

Service
4 Persons

Ingredients:

- 1 Cauliflower, medium & chopped into florets
- 1 cup Greek Yogurt, low-fat
- 1 Broccoli, medium & chopped into florets
- 1 tbsp. Olive Oil
- 2 Garlic cloves, minced
- 1 Onion, finely chopped
- 1 tsp. Dried Oregano
- 4 cups Vegetable Broth, low-sodium
- 1 tsp. Dried Thyme
- ½ tsp. Black Pepper
- Fresh Parsley for garnish

Method of Preparation:

1. Heat olive oil in a large pot over medium heat.
2. To this, stir onion and garlic, and sauté until softened.
3. Add cauliflower and broccoli florets to the pot. Stir and cook for a few minutes until the vegetables start to soften.
4. Pour the vegetable broth into the pot, ensuring that the cauliflower and broccoli are mostly submerged. Add thyme, oregano, black pepper, and cayenne pepper. Mix well.
5. Bring the soup to a boil, then lower the heat to simmer. Cover the pot and allow it to simmer for 15 to 20 seconds or until the vegetables are tender.
6. Blend the soup using an immersion blender or high-speed blend for 30 to 60 seconds or until smooth.
7. Spoon the Greek yogurt into the soup, making sure to mix it well. Adjust the seasoning if needed. Serve hot, garnished with fresh parsley if desired.

Tip:

- If you prefer a chunkier soup, blend it less.
- For added heat, you can add ¼ tsp. cayenne pepper.
- Taste the soup as you go and adjust seasonings to control flavor without relying on excessive salt.
- Add cooked quinoa or brown rice to make the soup heartier and increase fiber content.

- For a more filling meal, consider adding lean protein sources like cooked chicken breast, tofu, or white beans.

Substitution: Substitute low-fat sour cream or plain low-fat yogurt for Greek yogurt if desired. For a vegan version, replace Greek yogurt with a dairy-free alternative and ensure the broth is plant-based. You can use coconut milk instead of yogurt for a different flavor profile.

Storage: The soup will stay suitable for up to 3 to 4 days when stored in airtight containers in the refrigerator. When reheating, ensure the soup reaches a safe temperature of 165°F (74°C) to kill any potential bacteria. Reheat only the portion you plan to eat to maintain quality.

Nutritional Information per serving:

- **Calories:** 111Kcal
- **Carbohydrates:** 11.5g
- **Fiber:** 3g
- **Proteins:** 5.9g
- **Fat:** 4.8g

- **Sodium:** 188mg
- **Potassium:** 348mg
- **Calcium:** 110mg
- **Magnesium:** 46mg
- **Iron:**3mg

5. Asparagus & Lemon Grilled Chicken

This dish of grilled chicken marinated with lemon and served with asparagus is a perfect example of a healthy yet delicious meal that can align with the DASH diet. The recipe is easy to follow and provides an outstanding balance of flavors that will tantalize your taste buds. The combination of tender chicken breasts and crisp asparagus spears grilled to perfection is a treat for your senses.

Not only is this dish delicious, but it is also nutritious. Asparagus is a vegetable packed with essential vitamins, minerals, and antioxidants, making it an excellent addition to any meal. It is also low in calories and high in fiber, which can help keep you feeling full for longer, aiding in weight loss.

Chicken breast is another nutritious component of this dish. It is a lean source of protein that is low in calories and saturated fat. The DASH diet encourages the consumption of lean protein sources to support weight management, making this dish an ideal addition to a healthy meal plan.

When you combine asparagus and chicken, you get a meal that is not only delicious but also nutritious. The dish provides a good balance of carbohydrates, fiber, and various vitamins, contributing to overall nutritional balance and supporting weight loss within the DASH diet framework.

Prep
10-15 minutes

Time
25 minutes

Service
4 Persons

Ingredients:

- 4 Chicken Pieces, skinless
- 2 tbsp. Olive Oil
- 3 cloves Garlic, minced
- 1 bunch of Asparagus Spears, trimmed
- 1 tsp. Thyme Leaves, fresh
- Zest and juice of 1 Lemon
- Salt & Black Pepper, as needed

Method of Preparation:

1. Place lemon zest, lemon juice, olive oil, minced garlic, fresh thyme, salt, and black pepper in a bowl. Combine well.

2. Keep the chicken pieces in a shallow dish or a resealable plastic bag.

3. Pour half of the prepared marinade over the chicken, ensuring it's well-coated.

4. For optimal flavor, refrigerate the food in the marinade for at least 30 minutes. For best results, marinate overnight.

5. Preheat the grill to medium-high heat. Tip: Preheat the grill before placing the chicken to achieve a nice sear and prevent sticking.

6. Remove the chicken from the marinade and let any excess marinade drip off. Remove the chicken from the marinade and let any excess marinade drip off.

7. Cook the chicken breasts by grilling them for 6-8 minutes per side or until fully cooked. Tip: Using a meat thermometer to check if the chicken has reached an internal temperature of 165°F (74°C) is essential.

8. Coat the trimmed asparagus spears with the remaining marinade.

9. Grill the asparagus and chicken for 5-7 minutes, turning occasionally, until tender and slightly charred. Tip: Grill the asparagus until it's tender-

crisp, avoiding overcooking, which can result in a mushy texture.

10. Arrange the grilled chicken on a platter with grilled asparagus on the side.

11. Drizzle any remaining marinade over the chicken and asparagus.

12. Garnish with additional fresh thyme or lemon slices if desired.

Tip:

- To prevent sticking, brush the grill grates with oil before placing the chicken on them.

- Serve the dish with a side of whole grains, a green salad, or other vegetables to create a balanced and satisfying meal.

- You can add herbs and spices in the marinade, such as rosemary or oregano, to customize the flavor to your liking.

Substitution: Substitute chicken with fish fillets like salmon or tilapia for a lighter option. For a vegetarian alternative, marinate tofu or tempeh and grill until golden. If asparagus isn't available, try grilling zucchini and bell peppers for a colourful vegetable mix.

Storage: The grilled fare will stay suitable for up to 3 to 4 days when stored in airtight containers in the refrigerator. When reheating, ensure the chicken reaches an internal temperature of 165°F (74°C) to ensure it's safe to eat. Reheat only the portion you plan to eat to maintain quality.

Nutritional Information per serving:

- ➤ **Calories:** 111Kcal
- ➤ **Carbohydrates:** 11.5g
- ➤ **Fiber:** 3g
- ➤ **Proteins:** 5.9g

- ➤ **Sodium:** 188mg
- ➤ **Potassium:** 348mg
- ➤ **Magnesium:**
- ➤ **Fat:** 4.8g

6. Salmon Chowder

Elevate your weight loss journey with our flavorful and nourishing southwest salmon chowder. This hearty and satisfying dish is packed with nutrient-rich ingredients like salmon, vegetables, and a medley of spices. Furthermore, this chowder supports your weight loss aspirations and ensures you savour every bite. Incorporating lean protein, wholesome veggies, and heart-healthy fats makes it a perfect fit for those embracing a healthier lifestyle. Indulge in a bowl of this chowder, where taste and nutrition seamlessly come together, proving that achieving your weight loss goals can be as delicious as it is rewarding.

On top of that, bell peppers are low in calories while high in dietary fiber, making them an excellent choice for those seeking to reduce calorie intake. Alongside, bell peppers are naturally voluminous and can be incorporated into various dishes to add bulk without adding excess calories. This can help create satisfying meals that contribute to a feeling of fullness.

Prep
20 minutes

Time
35 minutes

Service
8 Persons

Ingredients:

- ¾ lb. Salmon Fillets, Skinless & boneless
- ½ of 1 Avocado, chopped
- ¾ cup Water
- 1 ¼ cup Low-Fat Milk
- 1 tbsp. Olive Oil
- 1 ½ tbsp. All-Purpose Flour
- 1/2 cup Red Sweet Pepper, chopped
- 1 ¾ cups Vegetable Broth, low-sodium
- 2 tbsp. Green Onions (white and green parts separated), thinly sliced
- 1 ½ cups 1/2-inch pieces Red-Skinned Potatoes
- ¼ tsp. Black Pepper
- 1 cup Corn, frozen, whole kernel & thawed
- ¼ tsp. Ground Ancho Chile Pepper or chili powder
- ½ tsp. Lime Zest

Method of Preparation:

1. First, wash the salmon fillets and pat dry with paper towels.
2. To poach the salmon, take a large skillet and fill it with water.
3. Heat it over medium heat. Bring the water to boiling.
4. Place the fillets in it. Return to boiling; lower the heat. Allow it to simmer for 6 to 8 minutes or until salmon flakes easily while keeping it covered.
5. Discard the liquid. Flake salmon into ½ -inch pieces.
6. Heat oil over medium-high. Add sweet pepper and white parts of onions; cook and stir for 3 minutes or just until tender. Stir in flour; cook and stir for 1 minute more.
7. Gradually pour in broth. Add potatoes, milk, salt, black pepper, and ground ancho pepper. Bring the mixture to a boil; lower the heat.
8. Simmer for 15 minutes or until slightly thick and vegetables are tender, stirring occasionally while keeping it covered.
9. Stir in the corn and cook for 2 minutes more. Gently stir in poached salmon and lime zest. Heat it through.
10. Top the chowder with the green parts of onions and, if desired, avocado, lime wedges, or additional ground ancho pepper.
11. Serve and enjoy.

Tip:

- If desired, garnish with chopped fresh cilantro and serve with lime wedges on the side.
- For added heat, you can add one chopped jalapeno.
- For added nutrition and flavor, include spinach, kale, or diced sweet potatoes to enhance the vegetable content. For added nutrition and flavor, include spinach, kale, or diced sweet potatoes to enhance the vegetable content.

Substitution: You could substitute salmon with other firm, flaky fish like cod or tilapia instead of salmon. Consider adding more vegetables or incorporating plant-based protein sources such as tofu for a vegetarian option.

Storage: The salmon chowder will stay suitable for up to 3 to 4 days when stored in airtight containers in the refrigerator. When reheating, ensure it reaches a safe internal temperature to prevent foodborne illnesses. It's recommended to heat the chowder on the stove over medium heat, stirring occasionally, until it's thoroughly warmed. Remember that the texture of some ingredients, especially vegetables, may change slightly upon reheating.

Nutritional Information per serving:

- ➤ **Calories**: 280Kcal
- ➤ **Carbohydrates**: 25g
- ➤ **Fiber**: 3g
- ➤ **Proteins**: 22g
- ➤ **Fat**: 10g

- ➤ **Sodium**: 287mg
- ➤ **Potassium**: 855mg
- ➤ **Magnesium**: 50mg
- ➤ **Iron**: 2mg

7. Sweet Potato & Mushroom Carbonara

If you're looking for a healthy and delicious alternative to traditional carbonara pasta, you may want to try sweet potato carbonara with mushrooms. This recipe swaps out traditional pasta for sweet potato noodles, which adds nutrient-dense fiber to your meal while reducing calories and carbohydrates. Additionally, the mushrooms in this dish provide a rich, earthy flavor and texture while being low in calories and fat.

The carbonara sauce used in this recipe is made with eggs, low-fat parmesan cheese, and seasonings, resulting in a creamy and indulgent coating for sweet potato noodles and mushrooms. The best part is that this sauce provides a rich and satisfying flavor without adding heavy cream or excessive fats, making it a healthy and balanced option for those watching their weight and heart health.

Moreover, sweet potatoes are known to be an excellent source of essential vitamins and minerals, making them a well-rounded addition to your diet. They also contain a high amount of fiber, which can help promote feelings of fullness and aid in weight management. Additionally, mushrooms are compatible with the DASH diet and are low in sodium, making them an excellent choice for those looking to support their heart health and control their weight.

Prep
10 minutes

Time
40 minutes

Service
5 Persons

Ingredients:

- 3 Eggs, large & beaten
- 2 lb. Sweet Potatoes, peeled
- 1 × 5-oz. package Baby Spinach
- 1 tbsp. Extra-Virgin Olive Oil
- ¼ tsp. Ground Pepper
- 1 cup Parmesan Cheese, low fat & grated
- Pinch of Salt
- 8-oz. Mushrooms, sliced
- 2 cloves Garlic, minced

Method of Preparation:

1. Heat a large pot of water over medium-high heat and bring it to a boil.
2. Cut sweet potatoes lengthwise into long, thin strands with a spiral vegetable slicer or julienne vegetable peeler. Tip: You should have about 12 cups of "noodles."
3. Begin by boiling the sweet potato noodles for 2 to 3 minutes, stirring gently 1-2 times until they soften but remain firm.
4. Reserve ¼ cup of the cooking water and then drain.
5. Return the noodles to the pot and turn off the heat.
6. Place eggs, parmesan, salt, pepper, and the reserved water in a medium-sized bowl and mix it well.
7. Pour the cheesy mixture over the noodles and gently toss with tongs until evenly coated.
8. Heat oil in a large skillet over medium heat. Add mushrooms and cook for 6 to 8 minutes, stirring often, until the liquid evaporates and the mushrooms begin to brown.
9. Spoon garlic and cook for one minute while stirring until fragrant.
10. Add spinach and cook for 2 to 3 minutes, stirring, until wilted.
11. Stir in the vegetables to the noodles and toss to combine. Season it with a generous grinding of pepper.

12. Serve and enjoy.

Tips:

- You can use cremini or button mushrooms for this fare.
- If desired, you can garnish it with parsley.

Substitution: You can use nutritional yeast or dairy-free cheese instead of parmesan cheese.

Storage: The fare can be stored in the refrigerator for 2 days in air-tight containers. It's important to note that the texture of the sweet potato noodles may soften slightly upon reheating.

Nutritional Information per serving:

- ➢ **Calories:** 312Kcal
- ➢ **Fat:** 12g
- ➢ **Carbohydrates:** 38g
- ➢ **Fiber:** 6g
- ➢ **Proteins:** 15

- ➢ **Sodium:** 587mg
- ➢ **Potassium:** 818mg
- ➢ **Magnesium:** 53gm
- ➢ **Calcium:** 235mg
- ➢ **Iron:** 3mg

8. Rainbow Salad

Rainbow salad is a visually appealing and nutritious dish with various colorful fruits and vegetables. The concept of a rainbow salad is to include fruits and vegetables in hues that represent the colors of the rainbow. Each color signifies the presence of specific vitamins, minerals, and antioxidants, making this salad a nutritional powerhouse. The dressing complements the freshness of the ingredients without overpowering their natural flavors.

Rainbow salad can benefit your diet, especially if you want to lose weight or follow the DASH diet. The diverse array of colorful vegetables provides a broad spectrum of vitamins, minerals, and antioxidants, promoting overall health and well-being. Additionally, the high fiber content of the vegetables helps achieve and maintain a healthy weight by *enhancing satiety and regulating blood sugar levels. Lastly, including various vegetables supports the DASH diet's emphasis on nutrient-rich, whole foods, contributing to a balanced and heart-healthy eating pattern.*

Prep
15 minutes

Time
0 minutes

Service
4 Persons

Ingredients:

- 1 Red Bell Pepper
- ½ cup Quinoa, cooked
- 1 Carrot, large
- ½ cup Crispy Chickpeas
- 1 Yellow Beet, medium
- 1 Broccoli Stem, large
- Parsley, chili flakes + sesame seeds for garnish, optional

For the Dressing

- 2 tbsp. Almond Butter
- Juice of 1 Lime
- 2 tsp. Rice Vinegar
- ½ tsp. Ginger
- 1 tsp. Miso Paste

For the Chickpeas

- 1 ×15 oz. Organic Chickpeas, Reduced Salt & low-Sodium, drained & washed
- Salt + pepper to taste
- 1 tbsp. Coconut Oil

Method of Preparation:

1. Preheat the oven to 375º F to 165 ° C.
2. Spread the chickpeas on a baking sheet and pat them dry with a paper towel, removing skins from the beans.
3. Melt the coconut oil and then rub it on the chickpeas. Season it with salt and pepper.
4. Roast the chickpeas for 40 to 45 minutes or until crispy. Keep them in the oven until it needs to be used.
5. Spiralize the vegetables using your spiralizer, cutting them into smaller noodles and adding them to a mixing bowl.
6. Stir in quinoa and toss to combine.
7. Mix the dressing ingredients in a small bowl and pour it over the noodles. Toss again to combine.
8. Transfer to two bowls and top with chickpeas.
9. Garnish and enjoy your Dash Diet Rainbow salad.

Tip: To get your chickpeas super crispy, allow them to sit in the warm oven for 1 – 2 hours

Substitution: You can use your choice of veggies in it.

Storage: The salad is best consumed the day it is made.

Nutritional Information per serving:

- ➢ **Calories:** 197Kcal
- ➢ **Fat:** 9.8g
- ➢ **Carbohydrates:** 23.1g
- ➢ **Fiber:** 3.6g
- ➢ **Proteins: 6.2**g

- ➢ **Sodium:** 96mg
- ➢ **Potassium:** 319mg
- ➢ **Magnesium:** 46mg
- ➢ **Calcium:** 28mg
- ➢ **Iron:** 3mg

9. Chickpea Salad

Elevate your taste buds and nourish your body with this chickpea salad, a delightful harmony of fresh, nutrient-packed ingredients crafted to align seamlessly with the heart-healthy principles of the DASH Diet. This wholesome creation combines mixed greens, juicy cherry tomatoes, crisp cucumbers, creamy avocado, and protein-rich chickpeas, offering a symphony of flavors and textures in every bite. Topped with a luscious Green Goddess Dressing featuring the zing of fresh herbs, this salad not only satisfies the palate but also embraces a commitment to well-balanced nutrition and culinary delight. Embrace the goodness of greens and wholesome ingredients with this refreshing salad designed to invigorate both your senses and your health.

Prep
10-15 minutes

Time
0 minutes

Service
4 Persons

Ingredients:

For the Dressing:

- ½ cup plain Greek Yogurt
- 2 tbsp. Chives, chopped
- ¼ cup Basil, fresh & chopped
- 2 tbsp. Lemon Juice
- ¼ cup Parsley, fresh & chopped
- 2 tbsp. Extra-Virgin Olive Oil
- 1 clove Garlic, minced
- Dash of Salt & Pepper

For the Salad:

- 6 Cherry Tomatoes, halved
- ¼ cup Pumpkin Seeds
- 4 cups Romaine Lettuce or Mixed Greens, chopped
- 1 ×15 oz. can of Chickpeas, washed
- 1 cup Cucumber, sliced
- ½ of 1 cup Red Onion, sliced

Method of Preparation:

1. Blend all the ingredients needed for the dressing in a high-speed blender for 30 to 50 seconds. Puree until smooth. Add salt and pepper as needed.
2. Place all the ingredients needed to make the salad in a large mixing bowl. Toss well.
3. Drizzle the dressing over the salad and toss gently.
4. Serve immediately and enjoy.

Tips:

- If using canned chickpeas, rinse and drain them thoroughly to remove excess sodium and enhance the salad's overall health profile.
- Toasting pumpkin seeds adds a nutty flavor and crunch. Consider toasting them lightly in a dry pan before adding them to the salad.
- Enhance the protein content by incorporating grilled chicken, turkey, or additional chickpeas for a more satiating and balanced meal.
- Add crumbled feta, goat cheese, or a dairy-free alternative for a burst of tangy flavor.

Substitution: Add or substitute vegetables based on personal preference. Bell peppers, radishes, or shredded carrots are excellent options. Similarly, Replace part or all of the olive oil with buttermilk for a lighter dressing.

Storage: The salad is best consumed the day it is made. But then, it can be stored in the refrigerator for 1 to 2 days in an airtight container. Store the dressing separately to prevent the greens from becoming soggy. Add the dressing just before serving. If possible, add pumpkin seeds just before serving to maintain their crunchiness. Alternatively, store them separately and sprinkle them on top when ready to eat.

Nutritional Information per serving:

- ➢ **Calories:** 304Kcal
- ➢ **Fat:** 8g
- ➢ **Carbohydrates:** 40g
- ➢ **Fiber:**12g
- ➢ **Proteins:** 22g

- ➢ **Sodium:** 400mg
- ➢ **Potassium:** 641mg
- ➢ **Calcium:** 420mg
- ➢ **Iron:** 3mg

10. Lentil Stew

Are you ready to indulge in the wholesome goodness of our hearty Lentil Stew with Salsa Verde? It's a comforting dish that combines lentils' rich, earthy flavor with the vibrant, zesty taste of herb-infused salsa.

This nourishing stew celebrates diverse textures and aromatic spices, bringing together the heartiness of lentils, the sweetness of vegetables, and the brightness of a homemade salsa verde. Every spoonful is a harmonious blend of protein-packed lentils, aromatic spices, and fresh herbaceous notes of the salsa, creating a delightful symphony that is both satisfying and nutritionally wholesome meal.

Plus, lentils are packed with plant-based protein and dietary fiber, which promote a feeling of fullness and satiety, aiding in appetite control and reducing overall calorie intake.

They're also low in calories and rich in essential nutrients, making them a nutritious and satisfying choice for those seeking weight management and adhering to heart-healthy dietary guidelines like the DASH diet. So, why not embark on a culinary journey with this stew? Every bite is an invitation to warmth, flavor, and the comfort of a well-balanced meal.

Prep
10-15 minutes

Time
35 minutes

Service
4 Persons

Ingredients:

- 1 tbsp. Olive Oil
- 1 Onion, finely chopped
- 4 cups Chicken Broth, low-sodium
- 1 ¼ cups Celery, finely chopped
- ½ cup Red Bell Pepper, finely chopped
- 3 Carrots, small, peeled & finely chopped
- 1 tsp. Ground Cumin
- 2 tbsp. Tomato Paste
- 5 tbsp. Shallot, finely chopped & divided
- ¾ tsp. ground Pepper, divided
- 2 cloves Garlic, large & minced
- 1 ½ cups French Green Lentils, sorted & washed
- 1 Lime, large & juiced

- Pinch of Salt, divided
- 1 small bunch of Italian Parsley, finely chopped
- 2 tbsp. White-Wine Vinegar

Method of Preparation:

1. Heat oil in a 4- to 6-qt. pot over medium-high heat.
2. Stir onion, celery, carrots, bell pepper, and 3 Tbsp. Shallot, and garlic.
3. Sauté for about 3 minutes or until softened, while stirring.
4. Spoon in tomato paste and cook for 30 seconds, stirring.
5. Add lentils, broth, ½ tsp. Pepper, cumin, and ¼ tsp. salt into it and mix well.
6. Bring the mixture to a boil. Cover, lower the heat to low, and allow it to simmer for 35 to 40 minutes or until the lentils are tender,
7. In the meantime, place parsley, lime juice, vinegar, and the remaining 2 Tbsp. shallot and 1/4 tsp. pepper and salt in a small bowl; mix well.
8. To serve, divide the stew evenly among 4 bowls and top each with a dollop of the salsa verde. Serve the remaining salsa verde on the side.
9. If desired, pair the lentil stew over cooked quinoa, rice, or a side of crusty bread to make it a complete and satisfying meal.
10.

Tips:

- Dice the vegetables evenly to ensure they cook uniformly. This creates a pleasing texture in the final stew.
- If you prefer a smoother stew, use an immersion blender to blend the stew partially. This creates a creamier consistency while maintaining some whole lentils and vegetables.
- Boost the protein content by adding cooked chicken, turkey, or sausage if you prefer a meaty stew.

Substitution: You can use brown lentils instead of French green lentils. Similarly, you can substitute chicken broth with vegetable broth or water.

Storage: This fare can be stored in the refrigerator in an airtight container for 3 to 4 days. Reheat on the stovetop or in the microwave until thoroughly heated, adding a little water or broth if needed to adjust the consistency.

Nutritional Information per serving:

- ➤ **Calories**: 322Kcal
- ➤ **Fat**: 5g
- ➤ **Carbohydrates**:.53g
- ➤ **Fiber**: 14g
- ➤ **Proteins**: 19g

- ➤ **Sodium**: 355mg
- ➤ **Potassium**: 1016mg
- ➤ **Magnesium**: 20mg
- ➤ **Calcium**: 28mg
- ➤ **Iron**: 6mg

11. Three Bean Chili

Warm up your soul with a bowl of delicious three-bean chili—a hearty and nutritious dish perfect for chilly evenings or cozy gatherings. Packed with a trio of protein-rich beans, an array of vibrant vegetables, shredded chicken, and a symphony of aromatic spices, this chili celebrates flavors and textures.

This recipe offers a versatile canvas for customization, allowing you to tailor it to your taste preferences or accommodate specific dietary needs. Whether you're a spice enthusiast, a fan of extra veggies, or looking to experiment with alternative proteins, this chili provides the perfect opportunity to get creative in the kitchen.

Prep	Time	Service
45 minutes	2hr 45 minutes	4 Persons

Ingredients

- 1 tbsp. Cumin Seeds
- 1 ½ Onions, chopped
- 1 tbsp. Chili Powder
- ½ of 1 Green Bell Pepper, seeded & chopped
- ½ tbsp. Paprika
- 1 bay Leaves
- 1 tsp. Dried Oregano, preferably Mexican
- 4 Sun-Dried Tomatoes, (not packed in oil), snipped into small pieces
- ¼ tsp. Cayenne Pepper
- 6 oz. Dark Beer
- 1 ½ tsp. Canola Oil, divided
- ½ lb. Chicken Breast, skinless, boneless, cooked & shredded
- 3 cloves Garlic, finely chopped
- 1 Jalapeño Peppers, seeded & finely chopped
- ½ tbsp. Unsweetened Chocolate, grated
- 1 dried Ancho Chiles, seeds and stems removed, snipped into thin strips
- ½ of 1 × 28-oz. can Plum Tomatoes, with juices

- ½ tsp. Sugar
- 1 cup Water
- ½ of 1× 19-oz. can Kidney Beans, rinsed
- 2 tbsp. Cilantro, fresh & chopped
- ½ of 1 × 19-oz. can White Beans, rinsed
- 1 tbsp. Lime juice
- ½ of 1 × 19-oz. can Black Beans, rinsed
- Salt & freshly Ground Pepper, to taste
- Nonfat plain yogurt, chopped scallion greens, and shredded sharp Cheddar cheese for garnish

Method of Preparation:

1. Toast cumin seeds for 1 to 2 minutes or until aromatic in a small dry skillet over medium heat while stirring,
2. Spoon it into a mortar and pestle and grind it to a fine powder.
3. Transfer the toasted cumin powder to a small bowl and add chili powder, paprika, oregano, and cayenne. Mix well; keep it aside.
4. Heat ¾ tsp. of the oil in a large, heavy pot over high heat.
5. Add chicken breast to the pan in batches, sauté until browned on all sides, and transfer to a plate lined with paper towels. Once cooked, shred them.
6. Lower the heat to medium and spoon the remaining oil into the pan.

7. Add onions and bell pepper. Cook for 7 to 10 minutes while stirring until the onions have softened and are golden brown.

8. Stir in garlic, jalapeños, sun-dried tomatoes, anchos chiles, and the reserved spice mixture. Stir for about 2 minutes until aromatic.

9. Pour the beer into the pot and allow it to simmer for about 10 minutes while scraping up any brown bits clinging to the bottom of the pan.

10. Add tomatoes and their juices, chocolate, sugar, bay leaves, and the shredded chicken. Add water and bring to a simmer.

11. Cover the pot and simmer, stirring occasionally, until the beef is very tender, 1 1/2 to 2 hours.

12. Add kidney, white, and black beans and cook for 30 to 45 minutes or until the chili is thick. Discard the bay leaves. Tip: Mash some of the beans against the pot's side to thicken the chili naturally.

13. Stir in cilantro, if using, and lime juice; season with salt and pepper to taste.

14. Serve with garnishes.

Tips:

- Rinse and drain canned beans before using to remove excess salt and starch.
- Serve the chili with a side of rice, cornbread, or tortilla chips for a complete and satisfying meal.

- To enhance the flavor of your dish, you can add ingredients such as cocoa powder, coffee, or a small amount of vinegar. These ingredients can add complexity and depth to the taste of your food.
- Add more liquid for a soupier consistency or less for a thicker chili.

Substitution: Use different varieties of beans, such as navy beans, cannellini beans, or garbanzo beans, to replace or complement the traditional three beans.

Storage: Three-bean chili can typically be stored in airtight containers in the refrigerator for about 3 to 4 days. You can reheat them on a stovetop or microwave. Add broth or water to achieve your preferred consistency if the chili seems thick after reheating.

Nutritional Information per serving:

- **Calories:** 358Kcal
- **Fat:** 8g
- **Carbohydrates:** 48g
- **Fiber:** 15g
- **Proteins:** 26g
- **Sodium:** 463mg
- **Potassium:** 949mg
- **Magnesium:** 55mg
- **Calcium:** 128mg
- **Iron:** 6mg

12. Thai Chicken Pasta

Thai Chicken Pasta with Peanut Sauce is a delicious fusion of savory, sweet, and slightly spicy notes that transports you straight to the heart of Thai cuisine. This culinary adventure combines tender slices of marinated chicken, an assortment of crisp, colorful vegetables, and a luscious Thai peanut sauce, all-enveloping a bed of wholesome whole-grain pasta. Perfectly balanced and remarkably satisfying, this recipe promises a delightful dining experience that is quick to prepare and easy to enjoy.

Furthermore, the whole wheat pasta fare is conducive to weight loss due to its balanced combination of lean protein, whole grains, and flavorful peanut sauce. It provides a satisfying and nutritious meal that aligns with weight management goals. The whole wheat pasta adds fiber, contributing to prolonged satiety and supporting a well-rounded weight-loss approach.

Prep
20 minutes

Time
25 minutes

Service
3 Persons

Ingredients:

- 3 oz. Whole Wheat Spaghetti, uncooked
- ½ cup Thai Peanut Sauce
- 1 tsp. Canola Oil
- 1 cup Chicken, shredded & cooked
- 5 oz. fresh sugar snap peas, trimmed and cut diagonally into thin strips
- 1 Cucumber, medium, halved lengthwise, seeded and sliced diagonally
- ½ cup Carrots, julienned
- Chopped fresh Cilantro, optional

Method of Preparation:

1. Cook the spaghetti according to package directions until al dente; drain. Tip: Cook the pasta just before you toss it with the chicken and vegetables to prevent it from becoming overly sticky or clumping together.

2. In the meantime, heat oil over medium-high heat in a large skillet.
3. Stir in the snap peas and carrots, and cook them for 6-8 minutes or until crisp-tender.
4. Add cooked chicken, peanut sauce, and spaghetti, tossing to combine until everything is well-coated and heated through.
5. Transfer to a serving plate. Top with cucumber and crushed peanuts, if desired.

Tip:

1. To make the Thai peanut sauce, mix 3 tbsp. peanut butter, 1 tbsp. rice vinegar, 2 tbsp. low-sodium soy sauce, 1 tbsp. honey, lime juice, 1 tsp. of each minced ginger and garlic and 1 tsp. sesame oil in a medium bowl with a whisker. Then, pour warm water gradually until the sauce gets the desired consistency.
2. Adjust the spice level of the dish by modifying the amount of red pepper flakes or by adding a bit of sriracha or chili paste.

Substitution: Swap chicken for tofu or shrimp for a different protein source. Similarly, you can use almond butter, cashew butter, or sunflower seed butter for peanut butter.

Storage: The Thai chicken pasta is best consumed the day it is made. In the refrigerator, you can store it in airtight containers for 3 to 4 days.

Nutritional Information per serving:

- ➤ **Calories:** 359Kcal
- ➤ **Fat:** 15g
- ➤ **Carbohydrates:** 43g
- ➤ **Fiber:** 6g
- ➤ **Proteins:** 25g

- ➤ **Sodium:** 300mg
- ➤ **Potassium:** 716mg
- ➤ **Magnesium:** 56mg
- ➤ **Calcium:**124mg
- ➤ **Iron:** 6mg

13. Spiced Salmon with Roasted Veggies

Spiced salmon with veggie fare is heart-healthy, combining succulent salmon fillets generously coated in a fragrant spice blend with colorful roasted vegetables. Bursting with vibrant flavors and nutritional goodness, this dish satisfies the taste buds and aligns with the DASH diet's focus on promoting heart health through balanced and wholesome meals. On top, salmon is an excellent choice for weight loss due to its high protein content, which boosts satiety, and its rich source of omega-3 fatty acids, which may enhance metabolism and support fat loss.

Prep
10-20 minutes

Time
20 minutes

Service
4 Persons

Ingredients:

- 1 lb. Salmon Fillet
- tsp. Dill Weed
- 1 tbsp. Brown Sugar
- ½ tbsp. Olive Oil
- ¼ tsp. Garlic Powder
- ½ tbsp. Soy Sauce, low-sodium
- ½ tbsp. Neutral Oil
- ¼ tsp. Paprika
- ¼ tsp. Ground Mustard
- Dash of Dried Tarr1/8agon
- ¼ tsp. Pepper
- Dash of Salt
- Dash of Cayenne Pepper

For the veggies:

- 2 cups Broccoli Florets
- 2 cups Cherry Tomatoes, halved
- 1 Red Bell Pepper, thinly sliced
- 1 Yellow Bell Pepper, thinly sliced
- 1 tbsp. Olive Oil

- 1 tsp. Dried Thyme
- Salt and pepper to taste

Method of Preparation:

1. Place all ingredients except salmon in a medium bowl and combine it well. Apply the spice marinade over the salmon.

2. Place salmon, with skin side down, on a lightly oiled baking sheet.

3. Grill for 10-15 minutes covered, over medium heat, or broil 4 in. from heat until fish begins to flake easily with a fork. Tip: Overcooking salmon can lead to dryness. So keep an eye on the salmon while it is getting cooked.

4. In the meantime, toss broccoli, cherry tomatoes, red bell pepper, and yellow bell pepper with 1 tablespoon of olive oil, dried thyme, salt, and pepper on a baking sheet.

5. Once the salmon is done and cooked, roast the vegetables in the oven for about 15-20 minutes at 300 ° F or 150 ° C or until they are tender and slightly caramelized.

6. Arrange the spiced salmon fillets on plates alongside the roasted vegetables.

7. Garnish with fresh lemon wedges and chopped parsley. Tip: Lemon wedges add a refreshing citrusy flavor and provide a dash of vitamin C. Squeezing

fresh lemon juice over the salmon just before serving can enhance the overall taste.

8. Serve warm and enjoy.

Tip:

- If you prefer more heat, add a pinch of cayenne or red pepper flakes.

Substitution: If salmon is not available or preferred, you can use other fatty fish such as trout, mackerel, or sardines. Alternatively, consider lean white fish like cod or tilapia. Substitute the salmon with tofu or tempeh for a vegetarian or vegan option. Marinate and cook the tofu or tempeh, similar to the salmon.

Storage: Salmon can be stored in the refrigerator in an airtight container for 3 to 4 days. Reheat in the oven or stovetop to maintain the texture of the salmon. Be cautious not to overcook the salmon during reheating.

Nutritional Information per serving:

- **Calories:** 256Kcal
- **Fat:** 17g
- **Carbohydrates**: 5g
- **Fiber:** 0g
- **Proteins:** 20g

- **Sodium:** 330mg
- **Potassium:** 319mg
- **Calcium:** 28mg
- **Iron:** 3mg

14. Mahi Mahi Tacos

This delightful recipe showcases succulent Mahi Mahi fillets, expertly seasoned and baked to perfection, nestled in wholesome whole-grain tortillas. Complemented with toppings bursting with vibrant colors and zesty flavors, these tacos offer a satisfying blend of lean proteins, nutrient-rich vegetables, and heart-healthy ingredients. Elevate your dining experience with a meal that not only tantalizes your taste buds but also contributes to your overall well-being. Enjoy the harmony of flavors, textures, and nutritional goodness in every bite, making this a standout dish for health-conscious taco enthusiasts.

Prep
20 minutes

Time
20 minutes

Service
3 Persons

Ingredients:

- 1 lb. Mahi Mahi, fresh
- ½ tbsp Chili Powder
- 1 tbsp. Avocado Oil
- Juice of ½ of 1 Lime
- ½ tbsp. Ground Cumin
- ½ tsp. Paprika
- ½ tsp. Onion Powder
- ½ tsp. Garlic Powder

For the Tacos:

- 6 Low-carb soft tortillas
- Shredded Low Fat Cheese
- Salsa
- Red onion, sliced or diced
- Tomato, diced
- ½ of 1 can refried beans, heated
- ½ of 1 Avocado, diced
- ½ of 1 can no salt added corn, drained and heated

● ● ●

Method of Preparation:

1. Spray a non-stick baking dish with spray oil. Pat the Mahi Mahi fillets dry with a paper towel.
2. Apply the fish fillets with avocado oil and then lime juice.
3. Combine the spices in a small bowl and then brush them over both sides of the fillets, ensuring they are evenly coated.
4. Arrange the fish fillets in a single layer in the pan.
5. Bake Mahi Mahi for 25 minutes at 425° F or 210° C.
6. Once the time is up, remove it from the oven and cut it into chunks.
7. While the Mahi Mahi is baking, warm the tortillas in the oven according to package instructions.
8. Spread fish chunks on the tortilla and top with the topping suggestions.

Tip:

- If you're into the sweet and spicy combination, chop up some mangos and pineapples and top with your favorite peach salsa.
- Select whole-grain or corn tortillas for added fiber, supporting the DASH diet's focus on whole grains.
- Include a side of quinoa or brown rice to make it a more substantial meal.

Substitution: You can replace Mahi Mahi with other lean fish like tilapia, cod, or halibut.

Storage: The fish can be stored in the refrigerator for 3 to 4 days in an airtight container. When reheating, make sure to heat it through.

Nutritional Information per serving:

- ➢ **Calories:** 309Kcal
- ➢ **Fat:** 11.1g
- ➢ **Carbohydrates:** 41.4g
- ➢ **Fiber:** 15.8g
- ➢ **Proteins:** 19gm

- ➢ **Sodium:** 396mg
- ➢ **Potassium:** 863mg
- ➢ **Calcium:** 242mg
- ➢ **Iron:** 11mg

15. Pan Seared Steak

This delectable recipe features succulent sirloin steaks, expertly seasoned with a blend of aromatic herbs, imparting a burst of flavor in every bite. The steaks are skilfully pan-seared to perfection, creating a golden crust that locks in the juices and tenderness. Balanced, nutritious, and incredibly satisfying, this dish embodies the DASH diet's emphasis on lean proteins and mindful seasoning.

Furthermore, this Pan-Seared Sirloin Steak recipe is conducive to weight loss due to its lean protein content, which promotes satiety, and its emphasis on flavorful herbs rather than high-calorie additions, making it a satisfying and nutritionally balanced option for those seeking to manage their weight.

Prep

20 minutes

Time

20 minutes

Service

4 Persons

Ingredients:

- 1 lb. Sirloin Steak, about 1/2 inch thick
- 2 tbsp. Olive Oil
- Pinch of Salt, divided
- ½ tsp. Ground Pepper, divided
- 5 sprigs of Thyme, fresh
- 4 cloves Garlic, crushed
- 3 sprigs Sage, fresh
- 1 sprig of Rosemary, fresh
- 1 lb. cups chopped Escarole

Method of Preparation:

1. Pat the steaks dry with paper towels to ensure a good sear. Coat the steak with ¼ tsp. pepper and salt. Ensure they are evenly coated.

2. Heat a large cast-iron skillet over medium-high heat. Tip: Ensure the pan is hot before adding the steaks to achieve a nice sear on the outside. Sear each side for a few minutes until a golden crust forms.

3. Place the steak on it and cook for 3 minutes or until charred on one side.

4. Flip the steak over and stir in oil, garlic, thyme, sage and rosemary.

5. Cook for 4 to 5 minutes while stirring the herbs occasionally, until an instant-read thermometer inserted in the thickest part of the steak reaches 125 degrees F for medium-rare.

6. Transfer the steak to a plate and top with garlic and herbs. Cover with foil. Once cooked to your liking, transfer the steaks to a plate and let them rest for a few minutes. This allows the juices to redistribute.

7. Add escarole and the remaining ¼ tsp. pepper to the pan.

8. Cook for 2 minutes while stirring often, until the escarole starts to wilt.

9. Thinly slice the steak against the grain into thin strips and serve with the escarole and crispy herbs.

Tip:

- Opt for lean sirloin cuts to align with the DASH diet principles, emphasizing lean proteins for heart health.

- Pair the sirloin steak with whole grains like quinoa, brown rice, or whole wheat couscous for a fiber boost.

- Add ground cumin and coriander to the seasoning blend for a hint of warmth and depth.

Substitution: You can marinate and sear tofu or portobello mushrooms with similar seasonings for a plant-based alternative.

Storage: The fish can be stored in the refrigerator for 3 to 4 days in an airtight container. When reheating, make sure to heat it through.

Nutritional Information per serving:

- ➤ **Calories:** 244Kcal
- ➤ **Fat:** 12g
- ➤ **Carbohydrates:** 10g
- ➤ **Fiber:** 8g
- ➤ **Proteins:** 26g

- ➤ **Sodium:** 394mg
- ➤ **Potassium:** 1111mg
- ➤ **Magnesium:** 60mg
- ➤ **Calcium:** 160mg
- ➤ **Iron:** 4mg

THANK YOU FOR FINISHING THE BOOK!

We would like to thank you very much for supporting us and reading through to the end. We know you could have picked any number of books to read, but you picked this cookbook, and for that, we are extremely grateful.

We hope you enjoyed your cooking experience and the delicious recipes you've tried. If so, it would be really nice if you could share this cookbook with your friends and family by posting it on Facebook, Twitter, or any other social media platforms you use.

We stand for the highest quality in recipe books, and we will always endeavor to provide you with high-quality, easy-to-follow recipes.

Before you go, would you mind leaving us a review? It will mean a lot to us and support us in creating more high-quality cookbooks for you in the future.

Please help us reach more readers by taking a few minutes to write a review.

Warmly,

The Lion Weber Publishing Team

Warmly,

The Lion Weber Publishing Team

IF YOU'VE ENJOYED

DASH DIET 2024 FOR BEGINNERS

Your Essential Guide to Healthy Living and Weight Management

YOU'LL ALSO ENJOY IN THIS SERIES:

MICROWAVE MUG MEALS FOR TWO

Enjoy More Time With Your Partner with these 50 Time-Saving and Easy Microwave Comfort Food Recipes

LION WEBER
PUBLISHING

SUPER SIMPLE

VEGAN MUG DINNERS

QUICK AND EASY
PLANT-BASED
MICROWAVE MEALS

LION WEBER
PUBLISHING

AIR FRYER RECIPES
FOR SMALLER HOUSEHOLDS

FRY IT UP
FOR TWO

LION WEBER PUBLISHING

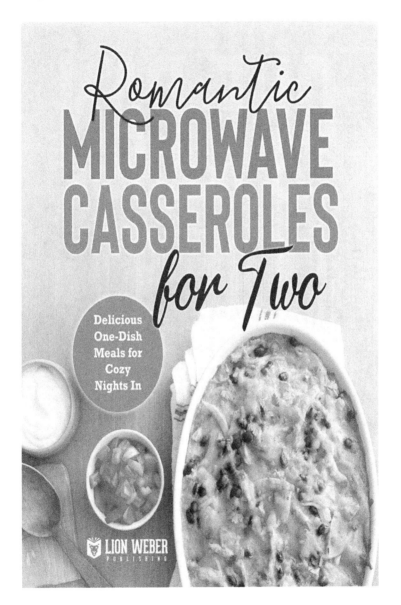

Thank you!

Made in the USA
Las Vegas, NV
03 September 2024

94735739R00083